Making Mission Possible

About CPAS

CPAS enables churches to help every person in the UK and Republic of Ireland hear and discover the good news of Jesus Christ.

Local church mission is the heartbeat of CPAS. As an Anglican evangelical mission agency we believe the message of the cross is real and relevant to all people, and that effective local church ministry is key to seeing men, women, young people and children come to faith in Christ.

We make mission possible by developing Christian leaders through leadership training, equipping churches with much-needed resources to help them grow, running 90+ Venture and Falcon holidays for thousands of 8–18s each year, and appointing evangelical leaders through our patronage work.

Our training for leaders includes the Arrow Leadership Programme (for leaders aged 25–40), conferences for clergy moving roles and training days and courses on topics relating to missional leadership, often in partnership with dioceses. We also offer courses for churches including *Growing Leaders*, *Mentoring Matters* and *PCC Tonight*.

www.cpas.org.uk

Facebook: facebook.com/CPASNews
Twitter: @CPASLeadership @CPASNews

LEAD ⏻N

*30 reflections to refresh and
re-energize your leadership*

James Lawrence

MONARCH
BOOKS

Oxford UK, and Grand Rapids, USA

Published by Monarch Books
an imprint of
Lion Hudson IP Ltd
Wilkinson House, Jordan Hill Road,
Oxford OX2 8DR, England
Email: monarch@lionhudson.com
www.lionhudson.com/monarch

ISBN 978 0 85721 864 3
e-ISBN 978 0 85721 865 0

First edition 2017

Acknowledgments

Unless otherwise stated Scripture
quotations are taken from the Holy Bible,
New International Version Anglicised.
Copyright © 1979, 1984, 2011 Biblica,
formerly International Bible Society. Used
by permission of Hodder & Stoughton
Ltd, an Hachette UK company. All rights
reserved. "NIV" is a registered trademark
of Biblica. UK trademark number
1448790.

Scripture quotations marked NLT are
taken from the Holy Bible, New Living
Translation, copyright © 1996, 2004, 2007
by Tyndale House Foundation. Used by
permission of Tyndale House Publishers,
Inc., Carol Stream, Illinois 60188. All
rights reserved.

Scripture quotations marked RSV are
from The Revised Standard Version
of the Bible copyright © 1946, 1952
and 1971 by the Division of Christian

Education of the National Council
of Churches in the USA. Used by
permission. All Rights Reserved.

Scripture quotations marked NRSV are
from The New Revised Standard Version
of the Bible copyright © 1989 by the
Division of Christian Education of the
National Council of Churches in the
USA. Used by permission. All Rights
Reserved.

Scripture taken from The Message
where stated. Copyright © by Eugene
H. Peterson 1993, 1994, 1995, 1996,
2000, 2001, 2002. Used by permission of
NavPress Publishing Group.

Extract p. 74 from The Servant Song by
Richard Gillard © 1977 Universal Music
– Brentwood Benson Publishing (Adm
capitolcmgpublishing.com/UK&Eire
Song Solutions www.songsolutions.org)
All rights reserved. Used by permission.

The publisher has no responsibility for
the persistence or accuracy of URLs for
external or third-party internet websites
referred to in this book, and does not
guarantee that any content on such
websites is, or will remain, accurate or
appropriate.

A catalogue record for this book is
available from the British Library

Printed and bound in the UK, June 2017,
LH26

CONTENTS

Keep watch over yourselves and all the flock
of which the Holy Spirit has made
you overseers.

Acts 20:28

INTRODUCTION

STOCKTAKING

Many years ago I worked in a factory. My role was to sweep the floors and paint metal girders. I worked alongside the man who was responsible for the stock room. Workers from across the factory would come to him to get a piece of equipment or an item they needed in order to progress their work. It wasn't a vast room, but I was always amazed at the extraordinary array of things within it, and his ability to find what was needed at a moment's notice. He assured me it was all down to good "stocktaking".

Once a month he would look back through his paper records (it was paper back in those days) of what had come in and out of the stock room. He would then check his records against what was on the shelves, and know what action to take in order to keep the stock room functioning well. And function well it did. It needed to. The production of machinery in the factory would quickly come to a stop if he didn't have the right stock in place for when it was needed.

Stocktaking: it is actually a practice we use all the time. When we open the fridge door to see what we have to eat for the week ahead, we take stock. When we check the fuel gauge in our car to see if we have enough fuel for the journey, we take stock. When we check the battery on our phone to see if it will last the day, we take stock. When we review whether we have everything ready for the meeting we are about to enter, we take stock. When we check our fitness app to see the number of steps we've walked through the day, we take stock.

Taking stock helps us to know both where we are – what we are currently doing, what resources we have, what we are prioritizing, how we are doing – and also where we might need to adjust something – what we need to give our attention, address, change, do.

A LEADERSHIP STOCKTAKE

Leaders know how easy it is, in all the opportunities that come our way and all the demands and expectations placed upon us, to focus on the activity of leadership and not to spend much time on reflecting on who we are, what we are doing, and how we're growing as a leader. It is easy for our stock to become low. While we may not measure this in terms of bolts and wrenches, we can measure it in terms of the two overall dynamics involved in healthy leadership: the inner and outer life of the leader.

The inner life is about the stuff most people don't see. Our prayer life, how we are dealing with a character flaw, our ongoing learning, how we are engaging with our emotions, how we handle failure, disappointment or conflict, our energy and stress levels, our exercise, drinking and eating habits.

The outer life is about the stuff many people do see. How we develop others as leaders, how we handle tricky conversations, how we turn ideas into action, whether we offer encouragement and thanks, how we enable those we lead to discern where God is leading.

These twin dynamics of leadership are reflected in the way Paul speaks and writes to others who share in leadership. In Acts 20:28 he encourages the Ephesian elders to keep watch over both themselves and the flock. In 1 Timothy 4 he encourages Timothy in a variety of ways to nurture the inner life, as well as faithfully and diligently fulfilling his outer life responsibilities. The inner and outer aspects of our leadership are inextricably intertwined, yet it can be helpful to tease them apart as we take stock of our leadership.

TAKING STOCK

Having worked with leaders over the last twenty years, I know how many of us don't give much time to a regular stock check. Then, when a particular challenge comes our way, be it internal or external, we may find ourselves without the resource for the next part of our leadership journey.

I wonder what a healthy and helpful stocktake would look like for you. The key words are "healthy", "helpful", and "for you". Don't take on someone else's way of doing it if it isn't helpful and doesn't aid health. But also be clear that not taking stock is only a short term option. Eventually we will be caught out.

In order for us to take stock regularly and intentionally it can help to have a daily, weekly, monthly, termly, and annual rhythm. This rhythm provides the context in which taking stock occurs. My own rhythm, developed over many years and constantly evolving, currently involves:

- A daily time of prayer and Bible reading. This includes journaling and a period of silence.

- Using a modified form of the prayer of Examen when I clean my teeth before going to bed (Google "Examen" to find out more).

- Several times a week starting my working day with forty-five minutes of reading.

- A weekly day of rest (Sabbath) from work, which ensures there is a pause in the busyness to rest, reflect a little, and press meaning into life.

- A six-weekly quiet day which includes, among other things, a review of the previous six weeks, and a prayerful thinking through of the next six.

- Two to three times a year meeting with my spiritual director (someone committed to helping me grow in my relationship with God who asks insightful questions to aid reflection).

- Three times a year meeting with a small group of three other guys (we've been doing this for over twenty years) where we listen to and for one another and offer encouragement and challenge.

- An annual stocktake at the start of the year when I try to identify what God wants me to give attention to in the year ahead.

In each of these rhythms there are different practices that facilitate reflection and action, that aid stocktaking. Do I always manage every part of this? No. Of course not. But the rhythm carries me along, and when I miss one aspect it isn't long before something else kicks in and re-introduces me to the pattern that I find helpful. Has it always looked like this? No. In the varying seasons of life it has looked very different, but over the years I have found what works for me. Does every leader do it in this way? No. Certainly not! Different personality types will approach this in different ways. But those who continue to grow and develop as leaders invariably have two things in common. They are intentional about taking stock, and they have found both a rhythm and tools that work for them.

Here are a few tips I've learnt along the way:

- **Be flexible** – what works now may not work in a year's time.

- **Try different things** – there are lots of ways of doing this (I've included some suggested resources throughout these reflections), so play with different ideas and see what works for you.

- **Ask others** – whenever you have the opportunity, ask other leaders what they do to take stock, to reflect on their own growth, and development as a leader.

- **Start now** – don't wait for the perfect time, or when you feel like it; make a decision today to start now.

- **Start small** – if this is a new thing for you, don't start with grand plans to introduce fourteen different ways you are going to take stock. Start with one small thing, and then over time build on it. Better to achieve a little well, than have a grand plan and for it to all collapse after a few weeks.

- **Share it with someone** – let someone else know what pattern you are putting in place and invite them to provide some accountability and encouragement along the way.

Taking stock doesn't sound very exciting, and many of us have inbuilt scripts we rehearse that mean we don't do it: "I haven't got time"; "there's too much to do right now, I'll get round to it later"; "everything is going fine"; "I'm not the reflective type"; "I know things aren't great, but thinking about them is only likely to make them worse".

However, without a regular stocktake the store room slowly empties itself of necessary resources, or doesn't contain new resources needed for new challenges that lie ahead. At one level stocktaking isn't very exciting, but that doesn't make it any less important. When talking with leaders who have had to take time out from their role due to stress or exhaustion, they often reflect that the balance between input and output, between activity and reflection, between doing and being, between work and rest, between drawing from their resources and replenishing their resources was out of kilter. A stocktake may have helped them to see that in time to prevent a crash.

USING THIS BOOK

Lead On provides a structured way to do a stocktake of both the inner and outer life. It invites us to reflect on how we are doing in thirty different areas of leadership. It can be used in a number of ways.

- For some that will be over thirty days, using one reflection each day.

- For others it may be over six weeks, using five reflections a week and two days to either catch up or spend time reviewing the week, exploring additional material, and deciding your action point.

- For some it will be over a longer period of time (a term or thirty weeks for example), with one or two reflections a week and then plenty of time to ponder the rest of the week. Or you may decide to allocate an hour a week to reflect on your leadership as a leadership discipline over a thirty week period.

Or you may choose some other way of using the material that works best for you.

HOW TO USE IT

The book is arranged into six sections of five-reflections, each section exploring five aspects of the inner or outer life of a leader. Inevitably there are a wide range of topics that aren't covered – leadership is a huge subject – and some will connect with you better than others.

Each reflection is structured in three parts:

- **Engage** – thoughts on an aspect of leadership to get you engaged with taking stock in that area.

- **Reflect** – questions to aid reflection on where you are at this time. You may like to use the space provided, or keep a journal or notebook (on paper or screen, although be wary of the temptation of clicking on to other things if you are using a screen) where you can explore your thoughts around the topic. Sometimes people are put off such reflective writing because they think it has to be beautiful prose. This isn't the case. You are writing for yourself, not for anyone else, so if bullet points, or random words across a page, or if drawing works for you, then that is the way to do it.

- **Explore** – suggested resources that might help you in your stocktake – books, podcasts, apps, videos, creative exercises, websites. Don't try to follow all of these up, but rather, when a particular topic or theme grabs you, take time to explore further.

You'll also find a leadership prayer at the start of each section, and a longer article to provide further stimulus at the end.

There are many different ways you can approach the material, but here are two suggestions to get you thinking about what will work best for you. Don't take these as prescriptive, simply illustrative.

APPROACH 1

If you are planning to use the material over thirty days or six weeks, on average it may take around fifteen minutes a reflection – five to read "Engage" and ten to "Reflect". If you decide you want to "Explore" further plan this time into your diary. You won't be able to take on everything that is raised either, so my suggestion is go with where the Spirit of God seems to be prompting or prodding you. For this reason at the end of each section there is a simple process to identify what action you are going to take as a result of thinking about the reflections in that section. Come up with one clear thing you are going to do.

APPROACH 2 (with thanks to Pippa Ross-McCabe for this idea)

Prayerfully choose a period of time (a week, a month, a term) during which you give priority to reflecting on your leadership. Start at the beginning and read through the reflections (the "Engage" sections) quite quickly, and only stop and spend time on reflecting and exploring further when your attention is caught or engaged (for example through intrigue, discomfort, or a sense of a big "yes"). For this approach the following guidelines may be helpful:

- Keep reading until your attention is caught.

- Stick with that particular reflection and engage thoroughly with all of it, including, where appropriate, the explore material and making decisions about actions. This may take fifteen minutes, it may take fifteen minutes a day for a week, or may become the focus of a whole quiet day or a retreat, or a conversation with others.

- Don't move on until you have "finished" with this reflection and are confident that you are ready to move to another.

You may only engage with a limited number of reflections during your allotted "reflection on leadership" period. That's fine. As with the first approach, go with where the Spirit of God seems to be prompting or prodding you.

WHEN TO USE IT

The material can be used at any time, but perhaps it may be most helpful...

- At a quieter point in the year when things are slightly less pressured, for example during the summer months.

- At the beginning of the year when you want to take stock ahead of the year to come.

- In one of those more reflective seasons in the Christian year, such as Lent.

- At the start of a sabbatical or extended leave as a way of identifying things you may want to give attention to through the rest of the sabbatical.

You could also use it with others in leadership, perhaps meeting once a week to discuss the latest section you've read and reflected on, supporting one another in your action points.

WHO IT'S FOR

The book is written for those who lead as a Christian, be it in your workplace, community, club, home, or church. My own experience of leadership is in churches and Christian organizations, and most of my work focuses in these two areas, so forgive me if most of the stories come from these worlds. I trust you will be able to make the necessary translation to your leadership context where necessary.

My prayer is that as you take stock of your leadership, you would know God's grace enabling you to be totally honest about yourself before him, God's strength for whatever leadership demands you currently face, and God's wisdom for decisions you need to make.

ACKNOWLEDGMENTS

Much of the material has been drawn from a monthly email called *Lead On* that I've produced for CPAS since 2012. It aims to be a brief injection of leadership ideas, resources, and reflections on the first Wednesday of each month. The longer articles in between each section were written for *Lead On* by a variety of leaders, and I am grateful for their permission to use them here. You will find a short description of each of the authors at the end of their article.

If you would like to sign up for the free *Lead On* email as a follow up to using this book, go to www.cpas.org.uk/leadon. You will also find a list of the links from this book on the Lead On page.

SECTION

1

THE INNER LIFE – RESOURCING YOUR LEADERSHIP

The exercise of Christian leadership is founded in watching over yourself: developing virtues, habits, disciplines and skills over a lifetime of formation, which undergirds and gives integrity to the leadership which is offered.

Steven Croft

A LEADERSHIP PRAYER

Lord, you have placed me as a leader.
You see how unfit I am to administer this great and
    difficult role.
Had I previously been without help from you, I would have
    ruined everything long ago.
Therefore I call upon you.
I gladly offer my mouth and heart in your service.
I would lead the people and I would continue to learn.
To this end I shall meditate diligently on your word.
Use me, dear Lord, as your instrument.
Only do not forsake me; for if I were to continue alone,
    I would quickly ruin everything.
Amen.

Luther (adapted)

1. ONE THING

⚙ Engage

Imagine. You can be granted one thing. Anything, but only one thing. Sorry, three wishes are out, just one. One thing. What would it be?

I write this in the middle of Lent, a season for reflection and repentance. It is a great opportunity as leaders, not simply to make the annual fast from chocolate or alcohol or whatever it is you normally give up for Lent, but to also reflect on where our deepest heart's desires lie.

One thing.

Those in leadership always have many pressing things they would love to see sorted. Right now, with a few months to go, we have no venue for three five-day residentials. The centre we've been using for the last fifteen years announced it was closing last Friday. That is one thing I'd love to see sorted.

However, important and urgent as many of these things are, Psalm 27 offers us a helpful reminder of one thing: "One thing I ask from the Lord, this only do I seek: that I may dwell in the house of the Lord all the days of my life, to gaze on the beauty of the Lord and to seek him in his temple."

One thing.

It wasn't what instinctively came to my mind. Yet... above everything else Christian leaders are called to remain connected to God, to grow in knowledge of who he is, to walk humbly and closely with him, to desire him above everything else. For the first priority of every Christian leader is not to be a leader, but to be a follower, a disciple of Jesus Christ.

Henri Nouwen summed it up well: "It is not enough for the leaders of the future to be moral people, well trained, eager to help their fellow human beings, and able to respond creatively to the burning issues of their time. All of that is very valuable and important, but it is not the heart of Christian leadership. The central question is, 'Are the leaders of the future truly women and men of God, people with an ardent desire to dwell in God's presence, to listen to God's voice, to look at God's beauty, to touch God's incarnate word and to taste fully God's goodness?"'

One thing.

Reflect

What draws you away from seeking God above all things? Why? What could redress this? What would seeking God above all things look like for you?

Explore

- *In the Name of Jesus*, Henri Nouwen (DLT). A short, profound reflection on Christian leadership that beautifully challenges some common assumptions.

- Take your journal or a piece of paper and write "one thing" in capitals, fairly large, in the middle and circle it. Over the next week or so write around the circle the things that help you to keep focused on the "beauty of the Lord" in the midst of everyday life.

2. STAYING FRESH

⚙ Engage

I am just back from a leaders' retreat where I've been speaking on the theme of staying fresh. It got me thinking. What help us to stay fresh and keep energized over the long haul of leadership?

There are many ways to answer this question, but I want to offer two suggestions that can help, the first of which we'll explore here and the other in the next reflection.

KNOW WHAT DRAINS YOU

In any role there is always a certain amount of stuff that we have to do that drains us. It is a great help to know specifically what it is that drains or hampers us from staying fresh. Obviously it will vary from leader to leader. For some it will be administration, for others ongoing people situations, for others certain meetings, for others conflict, and so on.

Make a list of such things. Take time to be comprehensive and specific – don't put "meetings" down, but the specific meetings. As you do this, you may also like to make a list of what brings you energy in your role (more on this in the next reflection).

Reflect on the list of things that drain you and see if you can divide them into three categories:

- Which do you simply need to recognize are part of the role and need to be done by you (and if you can find a way to make them a bit more fun or to do them in a more effective way all the better)?

- Which can you hand over to others who would be energized by them (sometimes this isn't possible because there is no one, but often there is)?

- Which could you actually stop doing because they aren't essential at this time?

Then take action on one of the items from the list; preferably one that is both relatively easy to do and brings a sense of relief. It is unrealistic to think we can eliminate all the things that drain us, but it is wise to know what they are, which category they fall into, and to balance them with the things that sustain us.

 Reflect

What does it feel like when you are drained? What are the symptoms you can spot as early warning signs?

⏱ Explore

- For a more nuanced way of reflecting on what drains and energizes you take a look at this blog post on managing your energy: http://careynieuwhof.com/how-managing-your-energy-can-make-you-a-far-more-effective-leader/

- Rest – a reflection on Psalm 23. Miriam Swaffield reflects on the place of rest in our busy world in this brief video: www.youtube.com/watch?v=pBXQgR0y8U4

- *How to Survive and Thrive as a Church Leader*, Nick Cuthbert (Monarch). Short pithy chapters offer practical advice on keeping going for the long haul as a leader.

3. STAYING FAITHFUL

 **Engage**

- -

Staying fresh and faithful rarely just happens. It requires some intentionality on our part. It helps not only to know what drains us, but also what sustains us.

KNOW WHAT SUSTAINS YOU

This looks different for different leaders, but some interesting research by Leslie Francis shows two common factors that help people keep going:

- **Maintaining a healthy pattern of personal devotion** – there is no set template for this, but we all know the danger of spending less and less time *with* God as we do more and more *for* him. Let's not get into a guilt trip, but why not take a moment to review your regular pattern of personal devotion? What one thing could you do to bring some new life into it?

- **Submitting our lives to others** – many leaders speak of isolation and loneliness. Ensuring that we have someone we are travelling with, giving an account to, who speaks into our lives, is known to help people stay fresh and faithful. Who might this be for you? A mentor, spiritual director, work consultant, friend, peer group?

Alongside these, I would also add:

- **Build on your strengths** – some spot strengths quite easily. They are the things that strengthen us, bring energy to us, the things we are wired to do. If you don't find it easy to know your strengths you may like to take Strengthsfinder (see Explore below). Sometimes we spend less time on developing these things because we can normally do them reasonably well without too much effort, but actually growth and development occur best when we focus on what we are good at, what energizes us.

- **Remembering our humanity** – Eugene Peterson writes "The problem for most church leaders isn't that they forget they are Christian, it is that they forget their humanity." Our humanity includes the need for a time of rest (the Sabbath pattern is hard wired into our humanity), time for key relationships, regular exercise, a healthy diet, and occasional injections of fun.

Inevitably there are seasons of struggle and difficulty as a leader. Yet, working out the balance between the things that drain us and the things that sustain us is part of how we keep going. We can survive for a while when we are spending more of our time doing what drains us, but not for ever. Ideally we will be in a 50/50 or 60/40 situation, where we are spending at least 50 or 60 per cent of our time doing what energizes us. I know in the corporate world they encourage you to aim for an 80/20 split, and that may be possible there, but for a variety of reasons I think it is unrealistic to be in much above a 60/40 split in most leadership roles in churches.

My experience is that I am constantly rethinking how these things interrelate in my life and leadership, and trying to work on the blend. I also know I am far less likely to survive, let alone thrive, if I don't give this some thought and time.

 **Reflect**

In your leadership role, when do you feel most animated, alive, energized? What percentage of your working time do you spend in these areas? How could you increase this percentage if it is currently less than 50 per cent?

🕐 Explore

- *Zeal Without Burnout*, Christopher Ash (Good Book Company). A short, honest book built on the premise "remember we are but dust", with very practical principles to live by.

- *Jesus Driven Ministry*, Ajith Fernando (IVP). An in-depth study of Jesus' ministry in Mark's gospel; particularly helpful as it is written from a non-Western perspective.

- *Strengthsfinder 2.0*, Tom Rath (Gallup). The book includes a code to an online inventory that helps you identify your top five strengths.

- www.strengthsfinder.com brings together various strengths-based resources.

4. LEADERS ARE LEARNERS

⚙ Engage

What is the place of reading in a leader's life? It appears a simple question, but it may be trickier than it looks.

Those who promote reading as an essential discipline suggest "leaders are learners". True – leaders are helped to stay fresh, keep engaged, and stretch their minds through ongoing learning. But does it have to be through reading?

What about podcasts, TED talks, conversations? Surely all these will suffice? And to be honest, in our fast moving and pressured lives, some of these are a bit easier to squeeze in. We can listen to a CD or podcast while we drive or go for a run, watch a TED talk on the train, or chat to someone while travelling to a meeting. Yes… but…

What about learning preferences? We know some are more kinaesthetic, others more auditory in their learning preference. Yes… but…

There is something about following a reasoned argument, grappling with a theological conundrum, engaging with an inspiring story in written form that adds something the other media don't offer so easily. I love listening to podcasts and watching TED Talks, but also know the discipline of ongoing reading is not to be laid aside too quickly.

Here are a few things that might help us in making the most of such a discipline:

- **Try to have a regular time so it becomes a habit** – better to read for just fifteen minutes than not read at all.

- **Be selective in what you read** – Steven Sample, president of the University of Southern California, points out that a choice to read one thing is a choice not to read something else.

- **Read beyond your specialism** – if you only ever read leadership books, or books on liturgy, or quantum physics, you may become rather narrow. My favourite book of this year has been about death and dying – *Being Mortal*, Atul Gawande (Profile Books) – and has both challenged me personally and also led to some great conversations with others.

- **Read different genres** – love biography? Have a go at poetry. Love contemporary texts? Try the classics.

- **Choose to read something theologically stretching** – I remember Lesslie Newbigin, theologian and missiologist, saying at the first lecture I attended at theological college that he always tried to have a particularly tough theological book on the go.

- **Work out a system to help access what you have read in years to come** – a system that has served me well for many years is to highlight as I read, then summarize each chapter briefly in the back of the book, and then write a brief review of the book on completion. It means I can turn to any book I've read and in minutes access the central argument, key themes, and good quotations and illustrations.

 Reflect

What sort of books do you naturally gravitate towards? Which books have had the greatest impact on your life? What might a healthy pattern of reading look like for you over the next year? What are the three books you are going to read next?

Explore

- Here are three different lists of leadership books to read:
  1. www.modem-uk.org/bestbooks.html
  2. www.fastcompany.com/3024245/leadership-now/6-must-read-book-recommendations-from-our-favorite-leaders
  3. www.lifehack.org/articles/productivity/15-best-leadership-books-every-young-leader-needs-read.html

- Alternatively Google "best leadership books". Or look at this blog post for insights into the reading habits of two billionaires: https://qz.com/668514/if-you-want-to-be-like-warren-buffett-and-bill-gates-adopt-their-voracious-reading-habits/

- Books for Life is a website set up by Krish Kandiah to promote reading. He interviews leading Christians on their top three favourite books and also offers a brief review of three latest releases in each video episode: www.booksforlife.uk

5. FINDING FUN

⚙ Engage

I wonder if I may ask a personal question. What does fun look like in your life at the moment? What brings a smile to your face, pleasure to your heart, a skip to your step, or laughter to your belly?

Don't press on until you've got an answer to the question.

Here is another way of considering this. If you look at your diary over the next three months, how many entries do you anticipate with pleasure because you know they are going to be enjoyable things to do or fun people to be with?

Leadership inevitably involves a fair amount of serious stuff: tragic life situations we share, tough decisions we make, complex issues to resolve. Leadership also tends to be full-on. It is quite possible to be buried in busyness, quite often "serious" busyness. In the midst of all this serious stuff, the idea of taking time out can feel frivolous or selfish. Or perhaps your issue is "there just isn't time".

If we're not careful all the fun goes. Symptoms might include the inability to laugh easily at ourselves and a longing for some of the pleasurable things we used to do (everything from the monthly trip to the cinema to the daily walk with the dog, from the day off with long-term friends to that hobby we really enjoy). Then we begin to lose perspective, begin to identify ourselves too closely with work, and begin to struggle under the pressure. This impacts those around us, especially those closest to us.

Maintaining some fun in our lives, some pleasurable activities, helps with sustaining ourselves and our leadership. There are seasons where the time and energy for such things is very limited, but be wary of a season becoming the norm.

Did you answer the earlier question? If so, does whatever you identified have appropriate space in your diary? And if you skipped over the question, or couldn't answer it, perhaps now is a good time to take a few minutes to review where the fun is in your life.

Reflect

What can you put into your diary over the next three months that you can anticipate with a sense of enjoyment? When will you put these things in your diary? What action do you need to take to make these things happen?

Explore

----

* An interesting blog post on work and fun:
  http://blog.kevineikenberry.com/leadership-supervisory-skills/why-leaders-must-consider-fun-as-part-of-their-job/

* And in this blog post the author explores three different categories of fun (challenging, accommodating, and relaxing) and why all three are helpful http://www.goodhousekeeping.com/health/wellness/advice/a18873/happiness-project-having-fun/

HOW DO WE KEEP GOING IN LEADERSHIP?

JOHN FISHER

THE DEMANDS

Leadership is demanding. There are demands from individuals in our organizations or churches, from structures, from wider institutions, and this is not to mention the demands from the busy personal and family lives we all live today.

For the busy, hard-pressed leader, life is a juggling act keeping all the balls up in the air without dropping any. When they do drop (and they do) that is when we tend to pause and reflect. We might ask, "What went wrong?", "How do I keep going?", "What motivates me?"

If we keep dropping the balls we have a problem. It can feel as if we lurch from one crisis to another, never quite in control of our own lives, or comfortable with the level of demand upon us.

In this section I want to suggest some ways to keep going as a leader, so we handle demands wisely and think strategically about sustaining our leadership for the long term. No one wants to drop everything and deal with the level of fallout this brings, so how do we keep going?

1. KEEP GOING WITH JESUS

When I first started out as an ordained leader my mentor, a clergyman in Bath at the time, gave me some advice. He said, "It is your relationship with Jesus that will keep you going, John." I have never forgotten those simple words and often bring them to mind.

I know when I am feeling down, or hard pressed, that my relationship with Christ must be the heart of my life. Whatever has happened I have always to focus on Jesus and take time out to re-connect with the Saviour and bring his grace to the situation.

Long term this personal relationship with Christ must be the driving force of our leadership. It needs our serious time and engagement at a personal level. Christian leaders are called to be people of deep spirituality. This starts from our own journey with Jesus and not from our place of ministry service, be that in gathered church or in some other aspect of life. I'm always amazed when I ask leaders how their journey with God is going how soon their conversation turns to their work.

Remember; we are disciples first and leaders second. If you need help with your discipleship then seek out support from a trusted source and be accountable for your relationship with Jesus.

2. KEEP GOING WITH TRAINING AND DEVELOPMENT

It is very easy to ossify in leadership. If we don't carve out time for learning new things, developing new skills, and meeting new people, we can very easily settle into a rut, which can be dispiriting in itself.

Making time for personal development is a must, as it brings a wider perspective and allows us to be refreshed and developed by other people. Use that training budget (if you have one) to its maximum and carefully plan time for new things into your diary. What training course have you recently completed, even if it is just a refresher?

I have been in my post a while now, but have booked onto a course in the autumn. This has taken much time out of the day-to-day demands, but it should pay dividends in the long term. I am really looking forward to it and am enthusiastic to see how it will serve my future work.

3. KEEP GOING WITH ADMIN

One Archdeacon I knew said to me that "good administration is thoroughly evangelistic". This was a comment that took me by surprise at the time. Admin is not the most exciting thing for me and sometimes we can use it as an excuse to bury our heads in the office or study away from other demands. However, if this is an area you find difficult then seek some practical help. Ideally find someone with a similar wiring to you who is good at admin and ask them how they do it.

It can be very liberating to have efficient admin processes in place that means you handle email, social media, phone calls, meeting paperwork, and so on quickly and well, and releases you to focus on other leadership responsibilities and wider vision. No one wants a leader sinking in admin.

4. KEEP GOING WITH YOUR PERSONAL CONTACTS

Too many leaders lose touch over time with valued family and friends. Often they don't realize this is happening until it is too late and damaged relationships are the result. Loving those who love us, care for us, and will support us when work is tough is worth its weight in gold. And if we are a local church leader, this also applies to contact with people outside the church. Too many Christian leaders know relatively few people in a meaningful way outside their organization or church. Is it time for you to join a local club because you want to and not for any other motive?

Nurturing your contacts and spending time with family is time well spent. Living on the job, for many leaders, unhelpfully blurs the boundaries of public leadership and private life. How is your public/private balance and do you need to redress it?

5. KEEP GOING WITH LEADERSHIP COLLEAGUES

Isolation is a real difficulty for those in leadership. We need to receive encouragement from supportive colleagues. If you are in a difficult leadership place where this support is thin on the ground then maybe it will help to look elsewhere. Can local leaders in other organizations or churches help, or offer support? To withdraw into our shell is not the answer and will leave us frustrated and resentful of the level of responsibility we bear. Leadership is best shared and a wise leader will grow and cultivate a team around them to share the load.

6. KEEP GOING BY LOOKING FORWARD

I recently met a minister who is just retiring from over forty years of very productive leadership in the same post. As I left I asked myself what was my abiding impression of this person and what had kept him going? My answer was simply that he kept looking forward to what God was going to do next.

It sounds simple, but he displayed an almost child-like quality of trust that the Holy Spirit would lead him and his community. He was also prepared to deliver the ministry to which he and the whole community were called. The result was he could point to at least four different phases in the life of the church, each one distinctly different. He finally came to the difficult decision that it was time for him personally to move on.

The lesson is to look forward. This is optimistic, positive, and important both in our work and for our personal circumstances. How long is it since you seriously assessed your future direction, or talked and prayed this through with a trusted adviser? Keep looking forward and be open to whatever new direction God may have.

John is Patronage Secretary at CPAS, working with churches and dioceses to appoint clergy to posts around the country.

ACTION REVIEW

THE INNER LIFE – RESOURCING YOUR LEADERSHIP

Reflect on section 1 using the questions below. Identify one thing you are going to do in response to what God has been prompting in you as a result of your stocktake so far. Remember, it is best to keep it as a simple and doable action.

What action are you going to take?

When and how are you going to take this action?

Who are you going to share this action with for support and accountability?

How will you incorporate this action into your prayer life?

REFLECTIONS

REFLECTIONS

REFLECTIONS

REFLECTIONS

THE OUTER LIFE – BACK TO BASICS

Too often we who wish to be servant leaders are little more than self-serving... Serving others, even those who reject us, is part of our Christian calling.

Jonathan Lamb

A LEADERSHIP PRAYER

Leadership is complex.
Lord give us wisdom.

Leadership is exciting.
Lord give us patience with those who are slow to follow.

Leadership is exacting.
Lord give us resilience to keep going.

Leadership is relational.
Lord give us love for those we lead.

Leadership is demanding.
Lord give us courage to face our fears.

Leadership is privilege.
Lord give us grateful hearts and thankful lips.

Leadership is nerve-wracking.
Lord give us faith to trust in you.

Leadership is influence.
Lord give us care to exercise influence graciously.

Leadership is serving.
Lord give us servant hearts to continually wrap a towel
    around our waist.

And in all these things,
may we rely on you and not ourselves,
follow where you lead,
and bring honour to your name.

Amen.

6. THE LEADER'S CHARGE

⚙ Engage

There are many pitfalls for those in leadership. Nothing new there. There always have been. Peter knew about some of them from personal experience, and in 1 Peter 5 offers some advice to the "elders among you". These are ancient words, but wise thoughts, and over the next three reflections I want to explore how they may help us be faithful and fruitful in our leadership.

> *Be shepherds of God's flock that is under your care.*
>
> **1 Peter 5:2**

REMEMBER WHOSE FLOCK IT IS

Peter is clear whose flock it is. God's flock. It is always God's flock. Leaders in the gathered church are never *the* leader. That position is taken. Jesus is the good shepherd, the flock belongs to God. We are always under shepherds.

For those who lead in other contexts, it helps to remember that God is still overall leader in the world. We cannot separate how we lead in the workplace from how we lead a small group on Wednesday evening. We are God's leaders wherever we find ourselves, ambassadors for the kingdom. It may not be his "flock" we lead, but it is his world, and the people we encounter are his creation.

Yet… our words may reveal a different dynamic. My leadership, my youth group, my ministry, my project. Of course we use it as short hand; we know it is really God's. But how easy it is for the language to become a reality; for us to subtly take "ownership" of the flock and to see it as ours. Symptoms may include increasing reluctance to trust others with leadership responsibility; our identity and sense of well-being becoming too closely related to how the flock are doing; and a growing irritation that people aren't doing what *we* want.

REMEMBER TO SHEPHERD THE FLOCK

The flock *is* under the elders' care. They have responsibility to lead the sheep to good pasture, to provide protection and care, and to find those who don't yet belong to the flock (see John 10). This is an enormous privilege and a serious responsibility as they work as under shepherds. Lazy, self-serving shepherds receive a stern rebuke in Ezekiel 34.

How do we hold these two realities together? Perhaps to acknowledge daily that the flock is God's, avoiding language that suggests otherwise, and to keep focused on whatever is core work for us in this time and place, avoiding the temptation of distraction and the sin of selfishness. For then we will be under shepherds who fulfil God's call on our lives, to tend the flock of God that is under our care with both humility and focus.

 **Reflect**

How might you change your use of language to reflect the reality that it is God's flock? What does "tending the flock" look like for you in this season? What might you need to address, give energy to, focus on?

Explore

- For those leading churches: *Working the Angles*, Eugene Peterson (Eerdmans). Pastor, academic, and prolific author Peterson calls those involved in church ministry to focus on three things: prayer, reading the Scriptures, and giving spiritual direction.

- For those leading in other spheres: *Good to Great*, Jim Collins (Random House), especially chapter 4. This is one of a number of excellent books by Collins, and focuses on insights learned from studying businesses that went from good to great over a sustained period.

- There are a range of apps available to help record how you are spending your time, often a good way to take stock of your current leadership practice. I know many have found "Timesheet" particularly useful.

7. THE LEADER'S MOTIVATION

 **Engage**

Be shepherds of God's flock that is under your care,
watching over them – not because you must, but because
you are willing, as God wants you to be; not pursuing
dishonest gain, but eager to serve; not lording it over those
entrusted to you, but being examples to the flock.

1 Peter 5:2–3

Why are you leading at the moment? Not what or how are you leading, but why? What motivates you in your leadership? Pause for a moment. What is the honest answer? Delve deep, search your soul, ask others.

Anyone who has been in leadership for a while knows how God honouring, kingdom serving, healthy motives can morph over time. Peter knew it as well.

Be careful, he says, of leading out of duty alone, rather than with a willing heart. Watch out for self-serving leadership, rather than other-serving. Check you're not enjoying power over others, rather than modelling Christ-likeness to those you lead.

Whilst we may think that our motives aren't visible, we are deceiving ourselves. Others pick them up. And even if they don't, wrong motives subtly destroy us and our leadership from within, robbing us of contentment and fulfilment.

I spoke with a church leader this week who has led with good motives over a number of years, and it is wonderful to see how the church has flourished under her loving leadership. I know she keeps a close check on how her inner world of motives impact her outer world of leadership. She has asked those around her who she trusts to comment when they see her acting from poor or misplaced motives. She meets regularly with her spiritual director and talks about such things.

Gladly exercising oversight, joyfully serving others, energetically seeking to follow Christ's example are part of good shepherding. If we find ourselves in a different place it may be time for meeting with a mentor (or equivalent), taking a retreat, or reviewing our role. For as Paul reflects in Acts 20:28, good shepherds not only keep watch over their flocks, they also keep watch over themselves.

Reflect

What motivates you in your leadership at this time? What has motivated you in the past? Who could you ask to help you keep a check on your motives?

Explore

• Write a prayer over a few days that captures some of the temptation for you around poor motivations and pray it regularly over the next six months.

• The Willow Creek Global Leadership Summit is an annual leadership gathering exploring a wide range of leadership topics http://willowcreek.org.uk/events/gls/ They also have a website with videos that capture some great insights. http://glsnext.com/index.asp

8. THE LEADER'S PERSPECTIVE

 **Engage**

- -

And when the Chief Shepherd appears, you will receive the crown of glory that will never fade away.

1 Peter 5:4

Christmas is a great season, but one of the things I find disconcerting is how easily it pushes out Advent, a season that reminds us of the second coming as well as preparing us to celebrate the first. And Christ's second coming is what Peter uses to encourage the elders to keep going.

Be encouraged, the chief shepherd will "appear". With so much tempting us to despair and hopelessness, it is good to be reminded Jesus will return. He has not given up on planet earth. He is still working his purposes out. If, as Napoleon suggested, leaders are "dealers in hope", for Christian leaders it is hope rooted in the coming of the king. One day, yes one day, all will be well.

Be encouraged, he is the "chief" shepherd. When we use the word "chief" we normally refer to the one who is in charge, as in Chief Constable. As the chief shepherd Jesus is in charge, holds things in his hands, is active in steering those under him. We can trust him and we can turn to him for help and advice on how to operate as leaders under his charge. His perspective is always going to be greater than ours. We are simply servants of the coming king.

Be encouraged, there is "a crown of glory that never fades away". All that hard work, all those tears and struggles, all that being misunderstood, all those decisions we make and can't publicly share the reasons for making them, all of that and much more will be worth it. For unlike the transitory crowns of this world, the crown of glory, of being with Christ for eternity, never fades.

Losing perspective is a common struggle in leadership. With our eyes focused on what is in front of us, what needs to be done today; with our hearts consumed by the troubles and hardships that people go through (and that we might be going through ourselves); with our minds captured by complex and weighty problems that need resolving, no wonder we lose perspective.

Peter would encourage us though to look up and look ahead. There is much about leadership that is hard, but we have a hope... one day, we have a help... the chief shepherd, and we have a reward... a crown.

 ## Reflect

Where are you struggling with perspective in your leadership at the moment? What would help you regain perspective? Who might journey with you through this?

Explore

* Failure is something we may try to avoid, but it is a part of the experience of nearly all leaders, and it can either break us or define us. In this blog post Jonathan Wilson reflects on how failure can bring freedom to leaders http://leadbysoul.com/leadership/you-are-not-perfect-how-failure-brings-freedom-to-leaders/?

* And for another perspective on failure try http://lifehacker.com/reframe-how-you-think-about-failure-by-changing-its-def-596193760

9. THE LEADER AND TRUST

⚙ Engage

Trust is an important factor in leadership. Like a tall tree, it takes time to grow, but can be cut down in a few moments.

Trust governs the speed at which one can move forward with challenging projects. Trust affects the way people receive tough words. Trust influences the level of collaboration within a team.

Reading Gordon MacDonald's helpful book *Building Below the Waterline*, I was reminded of how trust is generated. Trust builds with:

- **Consistency** – are we consistent in how we relate to people and live our lives?

- **Dependability** – are we a person of our word?

- **Openness** – are we honest in our communication?

- **Hard work** – are we prepared to put in the hours, to go the extra mile?

- **Impartiality** – are we equally available to the weak and struggling as well as the wealthy and attractive?

- **Longevity** – are we simply passing through or deeply committed to those we serve?

- **An ever deepening spirit** – are we growing more like Christ?

I might add trust also builds with a track record of competence, of people knowing that we can do the job. This begins with ensuring that we are doing the basics of our leadership role well. The basics vary according to the role, but if they aren't in place it is very hard for people to begin to build trust in us. There are generic basics for all leadership roles (for example being prepared to have tough conversations, personal organization that enables others around you to know they can depend on you to respond to emails or return a call), and there are specific basics related to the particular role we are in (for example, good classroom management for a teacher, good patient care for a senior nurse on a ward, or preaching for a church leader). Thinking through our basics and what competence looks like in our context is a great exercise to do early on in any role.

The opposite of trust is not "no trust" but "distrust", and the presence of distrust makes it very hard to lead. Time spent reflecting on how trustworthy we are as a leader is time well spent, and MacDonald's list is a helpful starting point for a sober assessment.

For whilst trust cannot be assumed or demanded, it can be earned and it can be graciously given. Then as leaders we have the wonderful privilege of people's trust, not to be expended on our personal projects, but on helping those we lead be about God's purposes in his world.

Reflect

What are the basics that need to be done well in your role? If trust is seen as a positive or negative amount in your leadership account, how far in credit or debit are you at this time? What would increase your trust credit balance?

Explore

- *Building Below the Waterline*, Gordon MacDonald (Hendrickson). MacDonald offers ideas on how to ensure the inner life is sturdy enough to sustain the outer life.

- *Leading with Trust*, Richard England (Grove Leadership Series No. 20). A brief guide to trust in leadership that builds on the work of Covey's larger book *The Speed of Trust*, available from the CPAS website.

- For a summary of *The Speed of Trust*, Stephen Covey, http://www. speedoftrust.com/How-The-Speed-of-Trust-works/book

10. THE LEADER'S COURAGE

 **Engage**

> *Ordinary courage is about putting our vulnerability on*
> *the line. After spending the past ten years interviewing*
> *people about the truths of their lives – their strengths and*
> *struggles – I realised that courage is not something we have*
> *or don't have, it's something we practice.*

Brene Brown

It was an extraordinary moment. Standing 128,000 feet above planet earth (that is 24 miles), Felix Baumgartner steps off the edge of his capsule and plummets towards the earth's surface, reaching speeds of over 800mph.

Through the marvels of modern technology we watch from a camera placed above him as he takes the terrifying plunge (search online if you want to watch it). My heart nearly stopped just looking at the video. Apparently his heart was beating at a normal rate.

Now some will think him completely mad (me, for example), others enviously wish they could have done it (my son, for example), but wherever we are on that spectrum, there is no doubting his courage.

Courage isn't the absence of fear. It is the ability to press on despite the fear, and it is an important quality in leadership.

Courage to do what needs to be done whatever the opposition. Courage to delay making a decision when everyone is pressing for it to be made, because you simply don't have sufficient information or time to make a wise decision. Courage to shape a community, school, factory, or church culture around gospel values, rather than allow the world's values to determine how you do things. Courage to challenge repeated unhelpful behaviour. Courage to resist the pressure to conform in a workplace when it will compromise your Christian faith.

Jesus exhibits such courage as he rids the Temple of money changers (Mark 11:15), as he talks with an outcast Samaritan woman at the well (John 4), as he challenges the prevailing view of leadership (Matthew 20:20–24), and as he presses on to the cross (Luke 22:39–46).

How do we develop courage? It's a combination of things:

- Gaining clarity about God's call. What is he asking us to do? The stronger this conviction inside the more likely we will lead with courage outside.

- Fostering shared leadership. Many of us are more likely to be courageous when we are leading with others and not on our own.

- Taking every opportunity to practise courage; making small courageous decisions now that bring strength to make larger courageous decisions in the future. Felix didn't wake up one morning and randomly decide to leap. He spent many years of his life making (initially smaller) courageous decisions that all led up to that big moment. Often these smaller decisions are made in our inner world.

- Praying for courage. It is striking the number of times leaders in the Bible need to be told to be courageous.

Lord, give us courage to follow where you lead.

☀ Reflect

Where can you exercise courage in your life and leadership today? What fears do you need to face? Which people may you need to lovingly challenge? What decision have you been putting off? What small act of courage now can help prepare you for the unknown bigger courageous act that is around the corner?

🕐 Explore

- *Daring Greatly*, Brené Brown (Penguin). One of a trilogy of books on Brown's core themes of vulnerability, courage, and shame. All are worth a read. To find out more visit www.brenebrown.com

- Take a large stone and using an appropriate marker pen write on it something that you know you will need to be courageous about in this season of your leadership. Place the stone where you pray as a reminder to ask God for courage.

TEN MISTAKES THAT LEADERS MAKE

JOHN DUNNETT

YOU'RE UNIQUE

There's no such thing as a definitive list of mistakes made by leaders. Each and every one of us is likely to have our own unique set. However, from my own experience in church leadership, and from observing leaders in many different churches and situations, I suspect that the "top 10" most commonly made leadership mistakes would look something like this:

1. FORGETTING TO ACT

I have visited many organizations and churches where they have obviously thought and prayed long and hard about vision – and have generated both lofty and godly aspirations – but have then believed the job to be done. In fact, the discernment of vision is only one stage in the process of enabling an organization or church to move into the things that God calls it to. Very often it's the second part of the process that is much more difficult – the development of a strategy and plans, questions relating to organization and re-organization, and the building of a culture that facilitates rather than undermines the vision becoming a reality. It was Sir Terry Leahy (previous CEO of Tesco) who said "execution is more important than having a good idea".

2. FOCUSING ON PROCESSES AND NOT PEOPLE

Related to this is the mistake that leaders often make when trying to initiate or further significant change. The management of the change process and the nurture of people in the process of change are well recognized issues in the commercial and public world but not so often recognized in church leadership circles. One of the most helpful writers on this subject is John Kotter (see *Leading Change*, Harvard Business Review Press 2012). His work in change management has led him to offer an eight stage "process" for leading significant change, and even if this is slightly too complex for most church situations, there is oodles of common sense and good advice in what he writes. Worth ten times the price of the book.

Mistakes three, four, and five are all to do with communication and can be summarized as: too much talk, poor questions, and under-communication.

3. NOT LISTENING ENOUGH

One of the things I observed about leaders is that there is often a tendency to talk too much (perhaps because they're good at it). We need to understand that listening to doubts, fears, and concerns is not a sign of weakness – rather of maturity and strength. The team meeting or Parochial Church Council that is dominated by the voice of the leader will be short on listening and often short on wisdom as a consequence.

4. POOR QUESTIONS

One of the things I have learnt from colleagues at CPAS over the past few years is the value of asking good questions. Sometimes questions need to be open and expansive so as to avoid premature narrowing of discussion or thought. At other times questions need to be precise and probing (see Emma Ineson's article later in this book).

5. UNDER-COMMUNICATION

I remember visiting a church a few years ago where I was told that the notice sheets were put out five Sundays in succession before they were re-written or thrown away. Crazy as it may sound, the reasoning behind this was that research suggests many people need to hear or see the same thing as many as five times over before "pennies drop" and they register the detail being communicated. In other words – we say something once and think we've been heard. Wrong! Important things need to be communicated repeatedly and in as many different ways as is possible.

6. CONFUSING THE URGENT WITH THE IMPORTANT

Mistake number six is to confuse the urgent with the important. Christian leadership often involves attending to the pastorally urgent – and we would always endorse the rightness of that. But let me give you a couple of examples of where I think the confusion may creep in.

- Most Christian leaders have a tendency to want to deal with the need or situation before them and feel less comfortable sitting back and praying or thinking about the middle to longer-term future. And yet this thinking is critical in allowing them to make a significant contribution to the shape, direction, and impact of the church or organization for which they have responsibility. Thinking ahead often feels unimportant at the time, and therefore gets shelved for the urgent. However, the reality could not be further from the truth. The farmer who fails to plough and fertilize reaps a poorer harvest than the one who does. In Christian leadership it is vitally important to ask questions about where we believe God wants us to be twelve months from now, three years from now, and so on. Such prayerful consideration is a unique and substantial part of Christian leadership and should never be continually shelved or ignored because of the urgent.

- We allow our sermon writing to be interrupted by incoming emails. If there is genuinely nothing more important than preparing to feed those in our care with the word of God Sunday by Sunday, then how can incoming emails possibly be permitted to distract? I make sure that Outlook is off when writing sermons, and I'm willing to bet that it's only once in a lifetime that there is something so important you cannot do the same.

When was the last time those you lead with took a day to pray and think about the future? When was the last time you took twenty-four hours to go "off-site", pray, and think about your own aims and objectives for the next twelve or twenty-four months?

7. MISTAKING A ROTA FOR TEAM

One mistake that is often not even noticed is to mistake "rota" for "team". A church or Christian organization that has well-prepared and presented rotas might believe that everybody is "singing off the same page". But the reality may be far from that. In a stimulating book entitled *The Performance*

Factor (Broadman and Holman Publishers), Pat MacMillan lays out the defining characteristics of teams that are working and relating well. He identifies the need to have a shared sense of vision, agreed and clear working processes and protocols, and several other key characteristics. It's not a book that is written specifically for Christian leaders, but it is a book that offers much to those of us who are called to Christian leadership.

8. AVOIDING TRUTH-TELLERS

A further and significant mistake that leaders sometimes make is to avoid "truth tellers". Proverbs 27:6 says "faithful are the wounds of a friend; profuse are the kisses of an enemy". Bible scholars interpret this to suggest that we all need friends who will tell us the truth about ourselves. This is doubly important for those of us in leadership – and the neglect or avoidance of it is a serious mistake. One question it can be helpful to ask ourselves every now and then is: "What has someone said or fed back to me recently that has caused me to stop something, start something, or change something?" If we're not able to answer that, it might just be that we are not open to the "wounds of a friend" and need to take more seriously being challenged, nurtured, and grown in our own leadership.

9. FAILING TO UNDERSTAND THE ROLE OF CEO

The penultimate mistake that many leaders make is to fail to understand the role of a CEO. In their seminal book, *The Leadership Challenge* (Jossey Bass), Kouzes and Posner suggest that CEO should stand for "Chief Encouragement Officer" rather than the more normal Chief Executive Officer. Those of us in the key leadership role (whether in a local church, an organization, a charity, or a project) need to understand that one of our key responsibilities is to "import" encouragement into the life and ministry of those for whom we have a responsibility.

In my former parish we had an item in each year's annual church meeting in which we awarded "T" mugs to individuals whose service during the previous year had been largely unnoticed but whom I believed should be acknowledged. It was a great way to point out (sometimes) unrecognized people. But more importantly the "T" stood for "thank you" and enabled us to say just that. There are many different ways to offer encouragement at different times and in different places. The critical thing is that we are intentional about doing so.

10. THINKING THESE DON'T APPLY TO ME

The final mistake is to believe that the mistakes above are those of others, and not mistakes you might be guilty of. So why not grab a cup of coffee, go back through this article once again, and give yourself a mark out of ten for each of the mistakes I have named. Then prayerfully identify which one or two areas of leadership you need to work on.

John is General Director of CPAS, regularly teaches on leadership, and currently has a variety of responsibilities within the wider Church, including serving on the Crown Nominations Commission (the group responsible for nominating Bishops) and chairing the Evangelical Group on General Synod.

ACTION REVIEW

THE OUTER LIFE – BACK TO BASICS

Reflect on section 2 using the questions below. Identify one thing you are going to do in response to what God has been prompting in you as a result of your stocktake so far. Remember, it is best to keep it as a simple and doable action.

What action are you going to take?

When and how are you going to take this action?

Who are you going to share this action with for support and accountability?

How will you incorporate this action into your prayer life?

REFLECTIONS

REFLECTIONS

REFLECTIONS

THE INNER LIFE – BUILDING RESILIENCE

Developing resilience is demanding, mostly done in secret, often humbling, not always fun. The pursuit of resilience never ends. It is lifelong calculated adventure.

Gordon MacDonald

A LEADERSHIP PRAYER

Lead me on, loving Father,
into all that you have prepared for me
and prepared me for.

Lead me on, empowering Jesus,
that I might serve your kingdom and fulfil your mission.

Lead me on, sending Spirit,
transforming me into all that you want me to be.

So that I might follow wherever you lead,
and trust you with whatever is to come.

Amen.

11. FIX YOUR EYES

 **Engage**

Leadership involves "oversight", and inevitably it is appropriate for our "eyes" to be drawn to lots of good and important things. However, it came as a helpful reminder to me the other day that the New Testament encourages us not to lose sight of two things.

Fixing our eyes on Jesus, the pioneer and perfecter of faith.

Hebrews 12:2

I am embarrassed to admit how much I need to be reminded of this. It is so easy to fix my eyes elsewhere. There are the obvious dangers of fixing my eyes on bad things, but also the more subtle temptation to fix them on good and even important things, but not the best thing.

The writer of the Hebrews will have none of it. Follow first, lead second. Fix your eyes on Jesus, considering him, "so that you will not grow weary and lose heart".

So we fix our eyes not on what is seen, but on what is unseen.

2 Corinthians 4:18

I also know how much I need to be reminded of this. If we live in the present without the light of the eternal we all too quickly lose perspective. For Christ followers it isn't possible to live well today if we lose sight of what is to come.

It always startles me that Paul can speak in this passage of "light and momentary troubles" when you think about all that he went through. But he doesn't lose heart (verse 16) because he has eternity in his sight.

What I hadn't spotted before is that both of these passages mention "losing heart". Most leaders have experienced the tentacles of discouragement as they wrap themselves around the heart, drawing us to focus on all that has not gone as we had hoped. It was John Stott, one of the most influential church leaders of the twentieth century, who confessed that discouragement, losing heart, was his greatest struggle in leadership.

In those seasons where we are perhaps a little weary and maybe losing heart, rest will be a helpful restorative. But so too is a bit of "eye fixing": perhaps a daily reading of a gospel to remind us of the Jesus we fix our eyes upon; or a daily prayer thanking God for what is to come that is unseen but eternal.

For the antidote to losing heart is not primarily a personal pep talk to get over it, but a clearer vision of Jesus and a deeper awareness of eternal things.

Reflect

When and how do you fix your eyes on Jesus? Each day? In a tricky leadership moment? In a season of affliction? When and how do you keep your eyes fixed on what is as yet unseen?

Explore

- *Don't Lose Heart*, Graham Archer (Grove Leadership Series No. 16). Based on some research among church leaders and a study of 2 Corinthians 4, Archer explores what saps the morale and what can be done about it. Available from the CPAS website.

- Print off Hebrews 12:2 and 2 Corinthians 4:18 (if you are arty, create a poster out of them) and place them somewhere you will see them regularly to remind you where to fix your eyes.

- *Encounters with Jesus*, Timothy Keller (Hodder and Stoughton). A great read to refocus us on Jesus.

- See also *A Resilient Life*, Gordon MacDonald (Thomas Nelson).

12. MANAGE THE PACE

 **Engage**

The best gift you can give the people you lead is a healthy,
energized, fully-surrendered, focussed self. And no-one else
can do that for you.

Bill Hybels

Few leaders ever reach the end of their to-do list, and even if they manage it, the nature of the role means that other things will quickly be added. One of the challenges for anyone in leadership is pacing oneself, finding rhythms that work, not constantly pushing hard.

One of my commitments is to deliberately slow the pace in those periods of the year when the pace slackens naturally. The research is clear: what leads to a lack of energy, emotional exhaustion or burn out is not stress, but the linearity of stress, where there is no let up, where it is constant.

For me, and for many in leadership, the summer period is a time to slow things down. Yet it is too easy just to continue running fast. It takes a deliberate choice, an exercise of discipline. I often have to say no to fun opportunities, resist the pressures to meet other's expectations. I don't find this easy, but I do know it is necessary.

Here are some of the things I try to do during a slower period.

- I work shorter days.
- I catch up on things that haven't been done (amongst other things, admin; for example the annual clear out of the filing systems – email, hard drive, and paper).
- I take time to think, pray, and prepare.
- I read more, relax more, sleep more, see a few more films.

- I spend more time with family and friends.
- I review my exercise and diet.
- I do some fun, energizing things.
- I take a holiday.

By the end I feel rested, renewed, and ready to re-engage with the next busy period. I also have another much shorter period in the year when the pace naturally slackens for a couple of weeks, and try to take a similar approach to that time.

If there is no such "natural" period in the flow of your year, it may be time to create one, to press one into your schedule.

The sabbath principle can be applied not only to a day a week, but also to a period in a year. Then we learn the unforced rhythms of grace that characterized the life of Jesus, and in our leadership reflect the one we follow.

Reflect

When in your year is there a natural slowing of pace? What are the things you can plan to do or not do in that time that will make it a restoring period for you? Why not make a list of possibilities today, and then choose a few and share them with someone who will help you to live them out.

 **Explore**

- *Finding Rest When the Work is Never Done*, Patrick Klingaman (Charlot Victor). Sadly out of print but available on second hand book websites, it addresses the problem of a to do list that never ends.

- Take a large piece of paper (at least A3) and mark off the months along the X-axis at the bottom. With the Y-axis representing pace, from "not at all busy" at the bottom to "flat out" at the top, draw the flow of your year. What do you notice? Ask someone who knows you well to look at your chart and offer any comments.

13. SPOT THE SIGNS

 **Engage**

----

*An intentional self-care on the part of leaders is not a
matter of selfish pampering, it is essential to maintaining
effective leadership over the long term.*

Peter Brain (adapted)

Most of us have them. Warning signs. Signs that we're pushing things a
little too hard.

For some it is the tell-tale bodily warning signs. Migraines, digestive
problems, aching joints, mouth ulcers, and so on.

For others it is the emotional red lights. Mood swings, angry outbursts,
sullenness, flirting with escapist sin, an inability to be patient with other's
problems.

And for others it is the tendency to indulge in particular behaviours.
Eating or drinking too much, pornography, endless watching of box sets,
duvet days, compulsive activity.

We're under pressure, and it is probably too much pressure. Of course,
every leader has those times when things are pressured. A genuine crisis,
a tricky relational dynamic, a complex project, and we respond by putting
in the extra effort and the extra hours. But if the pressure continues
beyond a season and becomes a permanent feature, then the tell-tale
warning signs develop.

Then what do we do?

- **Acknowledge them** – there is a tendency to ignore them, to press
  on regardless. Don't. That path leads to emotional exhaustion,
  growing disillusionment, anxiety, panic attacks, sinful activity, broken
  relationships.

- **Share them** – many of us don't like admitting weakness, but it is good to share what is happening with those around us. They can hold us accountable to do something about it, and may even be able to offer to help reduce some of the pressures. If necessary, we may need to seek professional help: a doctor, counsellor.

- **Face them** – it is unlikely the symptoms will reduce unless we face the cause, and the cause may be complex, deep, and multi-layered without a simple solution. However, a starting point may be to take time to reflect, to talk with others, and to pray. It is likely nothing will change if nothing changes, so a small step to start the process is better than no step at all.

Just as on a car dashboard a red warning light is not to be ignored, so too in our lives the tell-tale signs are there for a reason. May God give us self-awareness to know what they are, courage to face them, and his grace to find a way through.

Reflect

Imagine five rev counters on your life dashboard – emotional, physical, spiritual, relational, and intellectual. Being in the red zone of over-revving is not a healthy place to be in the long term, however much fun it may be for a while. How are you doing in each of these areas?

 Explore

----

- Complete a stress survey online, for example www.stress.org.uk/ individual-stress-test/, where there is also a lot of helpful information on stress.

- *Going the Distance*, Peter Brain (Good Book Company). Brain is a minister in Australia who researched why church leaders don't go the distance. Lots of great insights, including chapters for those who are responsible for the well-being of church leaders (denominational heads and local church boards).

- Here is a transcript of an honest and vulnerable talk given by Vaughan Roberts, a minister in Oxford, on leaders who last www.e-n.org.uk/2016/11/features/leaders-who-last/

14. TIME TO LEAVE?

⚙ Engage

A teacher approaches sixty and wonders whether they have one more job in them, or if they should stay where they are until retirement.

A leader has been in the same role for ten years and wonders whether they are stale, or even stuck, in the role.

A younger leader has been in post four years and it is tough, very tough, and they wonder whether to dig-in or move on.

Gordon MacDonald reflects: "Recognizing the right moment to leave is among a leader's most difficult decisions."

A moment's further reflection quickly highlights it isn't simply a matter of time in post. Some people are still exactly where God wants them to be thirty years into a role – faithful, fruitful, and flourishing. Others clearly need to move on after three years – frustrated, fractious, and falling apart.

MacDonald suggests eight signals that it might be time to leave (*Building Below the Waterline*, pp. 240–48).

- **Incompatibility** – good organization or church, good leader, bad fit.

- **Immobility** – no change over a long period of time, no willingness to change.

- **Organizational transition** – a growth point where a new kind of leadership is required.

- **Stagnancy** – a lack of personal development.

- **Fatigue** – when it reaches a chronic stage.

- **Family morale** – a spouse or child who is being harmed.

- **Closing and openings** – a sense that the time has come to an end or a new opportunity has God's fingerprints all over it.

- **The age factor** – simply no longer able to keep up with the pace that leadership demands in the role.

He encourages leaders who've been in post a few years to wrestle on an annual basis with the question of whether it is time to leave, seeking the counsel of others outside the situation, praying and fasting, and engaging in candid evaluation of their current position with those in their context. Wise words. There is not a rule-of-thumb for should I stay or should I go, but there is a Jesus we follow, and discerning his way forward and having the courage to follow is always the best option.

 ## Reflect

Reflecting on MacDonald's list, where are you in relation to time to move? Who will you discuss this with in your context on an annual basis?

 ## Explore

- *Leaving Well*, Andy Piggott (Grove Leadership Series No. 17). In his roles as CPAS Patronage Secretary and as an Archdeacon, Piggott has seen many people leave their roles, some well, some not so well. Read this short book to be the former not the latter.

- *Succession Planning*, John Fisher (Lead On article at www.cpas.org.uk/leadon)

- For perspectives on keeping going long term in a role see Ian Paul's blog post www.psephizo.com/reviews/how-to-sustain-long-term-ministry/ and *Long Obedience in the Same Direction* and *Should I Stay or Should I Go?*, Martyn Taylor (Lead On articles at www.cpas.org.uk/leadon)

15. APPROPRIATE VULNERABILITY

 **Engage**

----

*The hardest thing about being a leader is demonstrating
or showing vulnerability... When the leader demonstrates
vulnerability and sensibility and brings people together, the
team wins.*

Howard Shultz, CEO of Starbucks

At a recent gathering of leaders I was promoting the latest book in
the Grove leadership series. It's on vulnerability in leadership. A leader
commented: "That's interesting. I've never seen anything written on that
subject before."

It got me thinking. I was brought up as part of the generation who
were taught not to be vulnerable, to keep things to yourself, to "grin and
bear it". Yet our research into Gen Y (those born between 1980 and
2000, also known as Millennials) show they are looking for authenticity
in their leaders, and one of the ways they perceive that is when a leader
is vulnerable. Mention vulnerability amongst leaders and one will quickly
hear the warnings about being too vulnerable from some, and the
concerns about not being vulnerable enough from others.

The word "minefield" comes to mind, which is why I am grateful to
Emma Sykes for her perceptive and wise book on how to be vulnerable
as a leader.

She helpfully clarifies the difference between resolved and unresolved,
appropriate and inappropriate vulnerability, and then defines appropriate
vulnerability as the choice to relinquish power, and be open to potential
harm and risk through trusting in others, by revealing oneself in service
of the loving purposes of God.

In one of the most powerful examples of this sort of vulnerability
Jesus asks his disciples to pray for him in the garden of Gethsemane,

and they let him down (Mark 14:3–36). There are no guarantees when we make ourselves vulnerable. But without vulnerability we become strangely detached, distant, easily placed on a pedestal, and open to the temptation of believing we can get through it on our own.

Yes we need to be wise, yes it needs to be appropriate, yes it needs to be measured. But the invitation to lead in the way of Christ is an invitation to be vulnerable. What might that look like for us in the next month?

 ## Reflect

When were you last vulnerable with those among whom you lead? How do you feel about being vulnerable? What will appropriate vulnerability look like for you in this season of your leadership?

 ## Explore

- Brene Brown's excellent TED talk on the power of vulnerability www.ted.com/talks/brene_brown_on_vulnerability or for a longer exploration www.brenebrown.com/videos/

- *Vulnerability in Leadership*, Emma Sykes (Grove Leadership Series No. 24)

- *Engaging Gen Y*, James Lawrence (Grove Leadership Series No. 8)

- Get a glass jar and three different coloured pieces of paper (ideally, green, yellow, and red). Choose a period of time (month, term, six months, year) and every time you are vulnerable write it down briefly on a strip of the coloured paper (green for what felt like relatively easy vulnerability, yellow for more difficult vulnerability, red for really difficult high stakes vulnerability) and place it in the jar. At the end of your allotted time, take out all the slips of paper and review how vulnerable you have been and what you have learnt from the experience of different levels of vulnerability.

HELP!

RHIANNON KING

I am a big fan of asking for help. For years asking others for help has saved my bacon; getting me to places I otherwise wouldn't have found, getting me out of holes I would have languished in, and enabling me to understand things that, in different circumstances, would have baffled me.

But increasingly I realize how many find it hard to ask for help. We might know people who would rather double the length of their journey than wind down their window and ask for directions. Others would rather soldier on half the night clearing up, stacking chairs, washing dishes on their own rather than ask for volunteers. And Christian leaders suffer from this as much as anyone, needing help and not asking for it.

WHY NOT ASK FOR HELP?

So what's going on? Why is it that so many people find it difficult to ask for help? I guess there are a number of reasons:

- Many people live in fear of potentially upsetting or troubling others. What happens if they take offence at my request or they feel obliged to help when they don't want to?

- Some people would much rather just get on with it themselves, making sure the job is "done well".

- And for some it never even occurs to ask for help or, worse, they haven't realized or admitted to themselves that there is a problem which needs help in the first place. To ask for help sometimes means admitting that not everything is OK and that is a big step.

But perhaps one of the most common reasons is this: that many people see asking for assistance as a weakness or as an embarrassing sign of their lack of knowledge and skill, and few want this. Leaders, and particularly leaders in a new post, want to show others that they were wise to appoint them, that they can do a "good job". It is all so understandable.

The irony of it is that, more often than not, asking others for help is a display of great strength. It shows the strength of initiative (who can I ask?) and humility (this may make me look stupid or lazy or unimaginative) and flexibility (to be able to deal with whatever response we receive). From a leadership point of view, it can be an opportunity to empower others, and to develop others' gifts and confidence. And, of course, it can be an act of vulnerability, which is scary. But, as a friend of mine always used to say, "to stay creative in life we should do a scary thing every week".

A PARADOX

As a leader, there is a paradox (one of many leadership paradoxes) in the business of asking for help. We want to show others that they can have confidence in us, that we are able to do the job we've been called to; and yet we also want to demonstrate a level of vulnerability that shows others that we need them and trust them, and which builds relationship with them. It's a matter of balance between these two things – and that balance may be different for different people we interact with.

Jesus could have been a "one man band" but he chose to use the most fallible of humans to join him in his work and was never ashamed to ask for help.

Think, for example, of the practical help he requested in setting up for the last supper (Mark 14:12–16), or the water he asked for from the cross (John 19:28), or for the company he asked for in the garden at Gethsemane (Mark 14:32–34). It is this vulnerability which warms him to us, which makes him fully human. And he asked for help directly in his mission, sending out disciples in pairs for them to grow and learn, and to produce a team equipped for kingdom work in the future. And today God still shows the same trust in you, me, and everyone he calls to be involved in his work in the world.

I'm not saying that we should become lazy and always ask others before we've thought about an issue ourselves. Sometimes it's important to just get on with a job, but equally there is something quite special that happens when we become vulnerable and ask others to help us. We empower others, and recognize that they have gifts and skills or time that we might not have, and in doing this we build others up and are richer as a result, to say nothing of the piece of advice or practical help we have benefitted from.

It is not about becoming a church of indecisive disciples or an organization of ill-disciplined leaders. It is not about abrogating responsibility, but about having an eye for an opportunity to invite others in, whilst always respecting the "no"s and "not just now"s.

I work in a diocesan office and I'm always surprised by the relatively small number of clergy who choose to ask for help or who ask too late. It's sad, because asking for help is welcomed and can open all sorts of doors for a parish. If only clergy knew.

Asking for help flexes our humility muscle, achieves far more in the long run, reduces the chances of us being bottlenecks, helps us realize that we are not alone in what God has called us to, and reminds us that there are often creative solutions that we've not thought of. What's not to like?

TWO-SIDES

Lastly, remember that there are two sides to this equation and, amazingly, God has made a world where most people actually quite like to help. They feel blessed when they think they've helped others and it builds relationships. How win-win is that? And surely the same is true with God too. We know he loves it when we turn to him for help.

So next time you think you're going to go under with the volume of things you have to do or the weight of the leadership responsibilities that seem to have fallen to you... don't hang around. Ask yourself where you can go for help.

> Brother, sister, let me serve you
> Let me be as Christ to you
> Pray that I may have the grace
> To let you be my servant too.

Rhiannon is Director of Mission in Birmingham Diocese where she helps oversee many of their missional projects, and regularly asks for help.

ACTION REVIEW

THE INNER LIFE – BUILDING RESILIENCE

Reflect on section 3 using the questions below. Identify one thing you are going to do in response to what God has been prompting in you as a result of your stocktake so far. Remember, it is best to keep it as a simple and doable action.

What action are you going to take?

When and how are you going to take this action?

Who are you going to share this action with for support and accountability?

How will you incorporate this action into your prayer life?

REFLECTIONS

76

REFLECTIONS

THE OUTER LIFE –
THE LEADER'S APPROACH

*The goal of thinking hard about leadership
is not to produce great or charismatic or
well-known leaders. The measure of leadership
is not the quality of the head, but the tone of
the body. The signs of outstanding leadership
appear primarily among the followers. Are the
followers reaching their potential?
Are they learning? Serving? Do they achieve
the required results? Do they change with
grace? Manage conflict?*

Max DePree

A LEADERSHIP PRAYER

Lord Jesus Christ,
watch over those who are leaders.
Keep them faithful to their vocation
and to the proclamation of your message.
Teach them to recognize and interpret the signs of the times.
Strengthen them with the gifts of the Spirit,
and help them to serve others,
especially the poor and lowly.
Give them a vivid sense of your presence in the world
and a knowledge of how to show it to others.
Through Jesus Christ our Lord.
Amen.

From Catholics Online (adapted)

16. HIRED HAND OR WILLING WORKER

 **Engage**

> *How we talk about the people we serve and lead is not just*
> *a random choice of equally valid expressions. The rhetoric*
> *we use describes the kind of relationships that we believe*
> *we are involved in.*

Gordon Oliver

John 10:11–18 is a fascinating passage. In it Jesus describes himself as the good shepherd, and contrasts himself with the hired hand. The phrase that recently caught my attention is "he is a hired hand and cares nothing for the sheep" (10:13). By implication the good shepherd does.

Now I know leaders sometimes joke about the fact that leadership would be fine if it wasn't for the people, and that whenever anyone says this there are smiles and laughs because anyone in leadership understands what is being said. But, and this may be a big but, underlying the comment may well be a struggle that is a reality for many leaders – loving those we are called to serve. It isn't always easy.

How do we care for those we lead, especially when they are not following or behaving as we would prefer? Here are a few ideas:

- Remind ourselves that serving others is at the heart of Christian leadership. Those we lead are not there to help us fulfil our ideas and dreams; we are there to serve them in fulfilling God's work in and through them.

- Pray for grace and love. There will be many times when we struggle to love those we serve. We need divine help to bear the fruit of the Spirit. Ask for that help.

- Look for every opportunity to affirm and encourage people. Encouragement creates a positive culture.

- Get to know them. Listening to people's stories, hopes, fears, concerns, and motivations all helps in the process of knowing people, understanding people, caring for people.

- Forgive and forgive again. People do hurt us, undermine us, speak ill of us. Carrying hurt from others and ill feeling towards others can quickly degenerate into bitterness, and then cynicism.

- And in a church context, remember they are your brothers and sisters. Don't demonize them or speak ill of them, don't talk about them behind their backs.

No one starts off as a leader wanting to behave like a hired-hand, but many of us know the slippery slope that leads to this behaviour. Let's guard against it, and ask God to help us love and care for those we lead.

Reflect

Who are you struggling to love at this time? Name them and pray for them. Where has cynicism or bitterness (possibly the besetting sins of leaders) crept into your life? How can you root these out and replace them with something more helpful?

Explore

- *Do you love your people?*, David Banting (Lead On article at www.cpas. org.uk/leadon)

- In this blog post Stacey Reaoch reflects on how to love difficult people, www.desiringgod.org/articles/loving-difficult-people

- Identify someone you struggle to care for in your leadership. Place their name in the centre of a piece of paper. Prayerfully reflect on what Bible verse(s) God might be prompting you to live out in your relationship with them. Write them down around the person's name. Use the piece of paper as a prompt for your prayers over the next month.

17. DEFINING REALITY

 **Engage**

> *The first responsibility of a leader is to define reality. The*
> *last is to say thank you. In between the two a leader must*
> *become a servant and a debtor.*
>
> **Max DePree**

Every now and then it is good to remind ourselves of what we are about as leaders. Of course, there are dozens of leadership definitions, and hundreds of opinions on each of those definitions, so where to start?

Above is one I find helpful, and over the next three reflections we'll explore each phrase. To begin: "The first responsibility of a leader is to define reality."

Reality. Whose reality? And why is this the first responsibility?

In order to exercise leadership it helps to know how things are, otherwise we may well make decisions on the basis of information or ideas that are inaccurate. Defining reality is about daring to discover truth, to delve into emotions, and to discern perceptions. Courage is needed. We may well discover that the actual reality is far removed from our perception of reality.

Human beings tend to be expert at deluding ourselves, so defining reality is rarely done well on our own. It is normally much better to do it with others. Whether we are attempting to define the reality of our inner life as a leader (are we really growing in godliness?), or the reality about the outer life of the leader (are we really leading the team well, running great meetings, helping the process of discerning a clear sense of direction?), asking others to comment as colleagues, probe as mentors, coaches or spiritual directors, and challenge as fellow disciples is vital to the process.

Why not commit some time to be quiet with God, some time with those with whom you lead, and some time with those you lead, to ask them to help you define reality. A simple question can get the ball rolling: "Tell me, how do you see things?" Don't be defensive, don't react, just simply listen and engage. Further questions might include: if there is one blind spot I suffer from, what might that be? What are the things that others see that I am missing? What are people saying that we aren't hearing?

Leadership is about going somewhere, and if you want to go somewhere you need to know where you are starting from. Gaining an accurate definition of reality is often more complex than we imagine, so great leaders work hard at this, constantly probing, constantly looking for other's perceptions, constantly opening themselves to contrary viewpoints. Then, they carefully define reality in ways which people can grasp and keep themselves open to new information that may elucidate reality even further

 Reflect

----

How would you define your current reality? Who can you ask to inform your perception? When and how will you do this?

 Explore

----

- *Discerning Leadership*, Graham Cray (Grove Leadership Series No. 1). Cray explores how we discern God's direction in cooperation with God's Spirit and God's people, part of which is being clear about where we start from.

- Andy Stanley is the leader of North Point Ministries in Atlanta and is a well-known author and broadcaster on leadership. His leadership podcasts, which are freely available, cover a wide range of helpful topics. October and November 2016 are on discerning vision. http://andystanley.com

- There are a variety of community and church surveys that can be used to help "define reality". Here is a guide to a community survey by a Church of Scotland congregation www.presbyteryofannandaleandeskdale.com/communitysurvey.pdf. Natural Church Development is an extensive process for surveying a church's health, http://ncd-uk.com/. Search online for church or community surveys for more ideas.

18. SAYING THANK YOU

 **Engage**

Gratitude is the inward feeling of kindness received.
Thankfulness is the natural impulse to express that feeling.
Thanksgiving is the following of that impulse.

Henry Van Dyke

Saying thank you. My parents taught me from a young age how important it is to say thank you. Trying to do the same with my children when they were young was an interesting challenge. So why is saying thank you so important that it enters Max DePree's sentence on leadership?

The previous reflection considered the importance of defining reality, of naming how things are as accurately and clearly as we can. It provides the starting point for an attempt to shape things to be a little more kingdom oriented.

Saying thank you provides the ongoing energy to continue to move things in that direction.

Thank you expresses appreciation for effort, acknowledges contribution, affirms worth and value. Such small words, such big impact. Even more so if accompanied by a smile and good eye contact.

In *First Break All the Rules*, Buckingham and Coffman identify that one of the things to discover as part of an appraisal scheme is whether a staff member has received recognition or appreciation for their work in the last week. Why did they make this such a core question? Because their research revealed how little people received simple appreciation for what they have done, and how powerful such appreciation is in both motivating people and creating a healthy environment in which to work.

In my work I travel a lot, and often am preaching in different churches around the country. I try to make sure I say thank you to someone who has contributed to the Sunday event who might not normally get thanked. I am always amazed at the impact. How about every time we gather as the people of God, we seek to say thank you to someone? At the home group, the choir rehearsal, the PCC, the youth event. Or in the workplace, could we as leaders model thankfulness in our teams?

And if you have responsibility for others as a leader, what about making saying "thank you" your spiritual discipline for the year. For ultimately the more we say thank you, the more we not only encourage others but also remind ourselves of a God who is gracious and worthy of our thanks. As Paul wrote, "Be thankful in all circumstances" (1 Thessalonians 5:18, NLT): thankful to God for who he is and what he has done for us; and thankful to others for who they are and what they have done.

 Reflect

What would practising thanksgiving look like for you as a spiritual discipline? Who could you say thank you to this week? What would be the best way to say thank you?

🕐 Explore

- Do you remember star charts? How about creating one for yourself? Print off a calendar. Buy some stars. Every time you thank someone (not just think it) put a star on that day. At the end of a month you will have a very visual way of seeing how you are doing. Take a look at Brian Doyle's extreme version, saying thank you to someone every day for 365 days, www.youtube.com/watch?v=QNfAnkojhoE

- Laura Trice talks for three minutes on why saying thank you is so important. www.ted.com/talks/laura_trice_suggests_we_all_say_ thank_you?language=en

- *First Break All the Rules*, Marcus Buckingham and Curt Coffman (Simon and Schuster). Based on extensive research by Gallup, this book identifies what excellent leaders do to manage people well, and offers 12 questions as a basis for good people management.

19. LEADING AS A SERVANT AND DEBTOR

 **Engage**

Servant leadership is not an impossible ideal in our day.
Rather it should be the foundational cornerstone of our
thinking about spiritual leadership. Christ lived,
taught, and modelled it for us, and it is our true
distinctive as believers.

Stacey Rhinehart

Defining reality: helping those we lead to see things as they are. Saying thank you: expressing appreciation for what people do. In between, suggests DePree, a leader must become a servant and debtor. What does this look like?

Christians follow a servant king, one who came not to be served but to serve (Mark 10:45). The defining symbol of this sort of leadership is a towel, as Jesus took off his outer garments, wrapped a towel around his waist, and washed his disciples feet, a job not normally done by the leader but by the servant (John 13:1–17). Yet servant leadership is often misunderstood. For Christians it doesn't initially mean serving people, but serving God and through our service of God serving people; a subtle but significant difference.

Serve people and we end up becoming a *doormat*, dutifully doing whatever they think best. Serve God and we become a *doorway*, through which we enable people to walk into the priorities of the king and the purposes of the kingdom. Servant leaders serve God first, which means there will be times when we don't do what people ask, when we say no (see Matthew 20:21–28). Such leadership is often difficult.

For example, most of us would rather avoid difficult conversations – the team member who is bullying others into agreeing with what he wants. Perhaps he has been doing it for years, and no one has challenged his behaviour. The servant-leader plucks up courage, even when they would rather avoid the conversation, and does what is required.

Leaders are also debtors, those that owe something to someone else. Christian leaders are "in debt" to Christ for all that he has done for us and all that he invites us to share as leaders. This means we don't come to leadership with a sense of "right" or "entitlement", but rather responsibility and privilege. So the critical question for servant leaders isn't "what can I get from this?" but instead "how can I serve in my leadership role today that will further the purposes of the kingdom and bless others?"

Let's pick up our towels and serve.

Reflect

What is required in your leadership role at this time? How can you better serve those you lead?

 Explore

- The rule of Benedict has much on the place of the leader as servant and the importance of humility. www.osb.org/rb/text/toc.html#toc

- Take the word servant, write the letters down on a piece of paper, and think about a word starting with each of the letters that captures the heart of being a servant leader for you. Place it somewhere to remind you of your intention. If you lead with others, do this together, and then help each other live out your intention.

- Want to think more about servant leadership? Take a look at Greenleaf's website www.greenleaf.org/what-is-servant-leadership/

- There is an excellent teaching series called "Stronger" available from https://willowcreek.tv/archive/stronger/

20. PRAYING WITH PEOPLE

⚙ Engage

Christian leaders are expected to pray. When churches are looking for a Minister they often include in the person spec "prayerful". When we invite someone to lead the youth group, we want someone who prays. When we look to establish a CAP (Christians Against Poverty) money advice centre or food bank we want a leader who prays.

Maintaining our own personal spiritual life, including prayer, is vital to the well-being of the Christian leader. But there is another dimension – praying with people and not just for them. I've noticed in myself how easy it is to allow this dimension to go untouched.

A meeting with a colleague, and no prayer. A team meeting with a brief nod to God at the beginning and perhaps the end. Even a pastoral situation, and prayer strangely absent. If I am honest, I've particularly noticed this phenomenon when I meet with other clergy.

Why is this?

Embarrassment at not wanting to be seen as too pious? A faulty belief about our ability to achieve things? Over-busyness that subtly fuels the misconception that we are in charge? An awareness of the lack of praying with others in our personal life that spills over into our public life?

Many years ago I hosted some Christians from India. At the end of their visit I asked them what they had observed about English Christians. Their response was memorable. "You don't pray much with one another." I remembered my experience of being hosted by them in Vellore Diocese. We never left a home without someone praying; a PCC I attended spent a third of its time praying.

We pray for many reasons, but one important reason is to remember our dependence on God and affirm our belief that apart from him we can do nothing.

Of course, those whose leadership is primarily exercised in workplaces or community groups will need to exercise caution and operate within the constraints of their particular contexts. Yet even in these places there may be appropriate moments to pray *with* people, and certainly we will want to pray *for* people.

Leaders set the pace. A leader who prays with others models something core to the way we lead as Christians. So does a leader who doesn't pray with others. How about making this month a season of increased prayer not just *for* others, but *with* others?

 Reflect

If you find praying with others awkward, reflect on why that might be. What is at the heart of the struggle? What steps could you take to address these things?

Explore

- Many leaders create a prayer list of people they pray *for*, bringing a sense of order and discipline to their intercession for others. What would the equivalent be that would keep us alert to praying *with* others?

- See *PCC Tonight* (CPAS) for ideas on creative ways of praying within meetings, www.cpas.org.uk/church-resources/resource-for-pccs/

CREATING A GOOD ENVIRONMENT FOR VOLUNTEERS

SHARON PRIOR

In Ephesians we read that God appointed people to be "the apostles, the prophets, the evangelists, the pastors and teachers, to equip his people for works of service, so that the body of Christ may be built up" (Ephesians 4:11–12). As a church leader I see that my role is to manage and support the volunteers who serve in my church, so that the church will be built up. Those leading in other not for profit organizations where volunteers may operate will want to have a similar focus.

On my travels around the country training leaders it has become clear that most leaders see this as an important part of their role. Yet, almost all those I have spoken to say that due to busyness, the intentional support and management of volunteers tends to get put to the bottom of the to-do list.

Many church leaders also say that they struggle to get people to offer themselves for the various ministries within the church. I believe that these two things go together; if we give time to developing good structures that will value and support volunteers, then people will be more willing to come forward to serve.

So what can we practically do to make sure that people feel valued and supported in their service in the body of Christ or the organization they volunteer for?

1. GET THE THINKING RIGHT

Often when a church or organization employs a paid worker for a specific area of work, volunteers step back. I think this is partly to do with the fact that there is a misunderstanding of what paid and voluntary service is about. Paid workers are there to support the work of volunteers, "to equip his people for works of service". Therefore, it is really important that a leader prepares the organization for a paid worker and explains their role.

Volunteers are not there to support the ministry of the paid worker. They are there to work out the ministry that God has given them and to exercise that ministry in a team with others who also have a calling to that area. In this sense "volunteers" may not be the most helpful term. It implies that there are some within church life who go the "extra mile" and "volunteer", whereas, if we understand the Church as the body of Christ, all those who belong have gifts and skills to offer to help build the body. The paid worker is simply there to release these gifts and skills.

2. COMMUNICATE VISION

There are many avenues for volunteering nowadays. It helps to think through why someone would choose to volunteer at your church or organization. During the London Olympics the "Games Makers" were the volunteers who got a lot of media coverage because of their tireless and enthusiastic input at the event. The International Olympic Committee made it very clear through their vision that the volunteers were not just sweeping the floors, clearing up rubbish, or pointing people in the right direction – they were "inspiring a generation". So what is the inspiring vision that will captivate people to want to contribute in your organization or church?

In my experience it is the way the leader communicates the vision that actually makes the difference. So ask yourself "Why would someone choose to volunteer here?" and then communicate the vision accordingly. If people feel they are just filling a gap that anyone else could fill then they are less likely to offer their services.

3. COMMUNICATE VALUE

How do you feel valued in your organization or church? Is it by verbal encouragement or perhaps by an email or note from a member thanking you for your input? We all feel valued in different ways, so find out how your volunteers feel most valued and implement a strategy for developing this process within the organization or church. This will be caught if the leadership models it. We need to explain that volunteering is hard work, but the job would not get done without their input. We want volunteers to see volunteering as a commitment rather than a contract.

4. OFFER LOTS OF DIFFERENT OPPORTUNITIES

Have a wide range of realistic opportunities that people can volunteer for. In a church context it is important that nobody in the congregation is excluded, so find out what the gifts and abilities are of the individuals and look for an opportunity for them to serve. I used to lead an after-school club in my church (which was quite a small church, so there were not many people to volunteer). There was an elderly lady in a wheelchair in the congregation who wanted to help at the club, but could not see that there was a place for her. She thought she would, in her words, "get in the way". After talking with her it became obvious that one of her gifts was administration, so she came along and did the registration and birthday cards for the children. From feeling that she had nothing to offer, she became a key team member in helping the children feel loved and accepted.

5. LISTEN TO VOLUNTEERS

I know this may sound obvious, but when we are really busy it is easy just to take volunteers for granted. It is important to give volunteers a voice in the development of strategy and policymaking. This will help them to "buy in" to the work of an organization or the ministry of a church. Listen to what makes them feel good about volunteering and what makes them unhappy. In my experience volunteers generally do not complain if they are unhappy, they just walk away.

So for those who are leaders creating a great volunteering environment, it helps to:

- Teach about the importance of volunteering to build up the body of Christ.

- Connect to their ministry by finding out what motivates them to volunteer.

- Train them to be even better in their volunteering role.

- Sustain them in ministry by valuing them and showing appreciation.

A WAY FORWARD

I find it helpful to remember four Cs when leading volunteers:

- **Create** an environment that they will enjoy.

- **Community** is the glue for retention of volunteers – help them to feel they belong.

- **Celebrate** all the ways that you see God using the volunteer teams.

- **Commend** them for their involvement – we need to create an inspirational environment.

Perhaps it would be a good idea to reflect on the points above with those you share leadership with in your organization or church and identify a realistic way forward. Teamwork is the key here, as the overall leader cannot do everything listed above on their own, and in most not for profit and church contexts some of those in the team are likely to be volunteers.

Sharon is a senior tutor at Moorlands College and part-time church leader at Iford Baptist Church.

ACTION REVIEW

THE OUTER LIFE – THE LEADER'S APPROACH

Reflect on section 4 using the questions below. Identify one thing you are going to do in response to what God has been prompting in you as a result of your stocktake so far. Remember, it is best to keep it as a simple and doable action.

What action are you going to take?

When and how are you going to take this action?

Who are you going to share this action with for support and accountability?

How will you incorporate this action into your prayer life?

REFLECTIONS

REFLECTIONS

THE INNER LIFE – ESTABLISHING RHYTHMS

We can't run our lives without some sort of approach to getting things done. The issue is not whether we have an approach to personal productivity; the issue is whether our approach is a good one or a bad one.

Matt Perman

A LEADERSHIP PRAYER

Lord, thank you for your call on my life.
Grow me in maturity, that I may be steadfast.
Grow me in vision that I may be passionate.
Grow me in trust, that I may relinquish control.
Grow me in love, that I may see people as you do.
Grow me in playfulness, that I may relax and laugh.
Grow me in leadership, that I may serve your kingdom
  purposes.
In the name of the Father, the Son, and the Holy Spirit.
Amen.

21. CHOOSING WHAT TO DO

 **Engage**

- -

There will always be more good ideas than there is capacity to execute.

Chris McChesney

It's the start of the day and you're looking at your to do list wondering which items to prioritize. It's the start of the week and you're looking at your diary and considering what can be added to your already busy schedule. It's the start of the term and you're thinking about priorities and how many new projects you can start over the next three months.

What to do?

Some are very easy to decide. Those things that are going to take just a minute or two can often be done now. And those that require an hour or two can be put in the diary. But others, those projects that require concerted effort and time, are much trickier. The likelihood is that we have more things we could do than we have time or energy to do them.

What to do?

Choose. Choose wisely. For every choice to do something is a choice to not do something else. And how do we choose wisely? Involve others, take time, and select carefully:

- **Involving others** means we gain the perspective, preference, and passion from people who don't see things as we do.

- **Taking time** means things can percolate; we can pray, consider unintended consequences, and sift through multiple options.

- **Select carefully** means we don't necessarily go for the obvious or the glamorous, but hear God's voice to serve others, care for the outcast, reflect the values of the kingdom.

Leadership involves many choices, and we won't always get them right. But choosing wisely where we invest time, energy, and resources will lead to things changing, developing, even flourishing. Often we can look back on something good that has happened through our leadership and return to a choice we made, sometimes years before, to do this and not that.

A colleague gaining promotion. We made a choice six months ago – to invest in their development. A CAP project established in the community. We made a choice two years ago – to work with others in our area to care for those struggling with debt. A young person being baptized as a new believer. We made a choice four years ago – to focus on nurturing connections with non-churched teenagers in the local school.

May God help us to choose wisely by involving others, taking time, and selecting carefully.

 Reflect

What choices lie before you? Who can you involve? What's your timescale? How will you decide?

 Explore

- Watch Chris McChesney's talk at the Willow Creek GLS 2016 on "Execution", available from www.willowcreek.org.uk/product/global-leadership-summit-2016-team-edition-dvd/

- There are numerous books on ordering our lives, here are a few I've found particularly helpful: *Beyond Busyness*, Stephen Cherry (Sacristy Press); *Do It Tomorrow*, Mark Forster (Hodder); *Busy Christian Living*, Emma Ineson (Continuum); *The Busy Christian's Guide to Busyness*, Tim Chester (IVP); *What's Best Next*, Matt Perman (Zondervan); *Time for Everything*, Matt Fuller (Good Book Company); *Ordering Your Private World*, Gordon MacDonald (Thomas Nelson). How about reading one a year over the next few years as a way of reflecting on ordering your life well? As a starting point, pick one to work through in the coming months.

22. STOPPING, PAUSING, REFLECTING

 **Engage**

- -

An unexamined life is not worth living.

Socrates

Leaders tend to be future oriented. There are things to be done, places to go, people to see. We're not always good at stopping, pausing, reflecting.

As I mentioned in the introduction, over many years I have developed a discipline that I have found helpful. At six weekly intervals I take some time to stop, pause, and reflect. And at one point in the year (for me this is in January) I take some time out to review things in a more thorough way. It normally involves a quiet day away from the phone and email, some time to pray, and a series of questions to reflect on.

I realize I am in a privileged position where I can do this as part of my role, and whilst I understand that not all leaders can, it is also true that many who could, don't. Every time one of these periods to pause comes up, I find there are enormous pressures to miss it. But I've learnt over the years that to succumb to the pressure of the immediate is a big mistake. I can literally measure my spiritual, emotional, and relational well-being against the consistency of taking these times to stop, pause, and reflect. And to be transparent, do I always manage to take them? No – on average I miss one a year, but if they weren't in the diary at all I wouldn't make any of them.

The purpose of these periods of stopping? Twofold: to embrace what has been, and discern what may be.

- **Looking back** is a great way of pressing meaning into life. Without reflection we are unlikely to learn from the past. We might also miss something God is doing. We are in danger of skimming over the endless commitments without any sense of gratitude to God and appropriate satisfaction in work done. In looking back we may become aware of things we need to confess, people it would be good to approach and say sorry to, or things we can amend.

- **Looking forward** helps us to spot where God might be leading, to pick up on the gentle nudge of the Spirit – a character issue he wishes to address, a leadership competency we need to develop, a relationship we need to give more time to, a project we need to start, tweak or abandon.

In all of this there is a fresh sense of dedicating oneself in his service, powerfully caught in the Methodist covenant service prayer of surrender. For at the end of the day there is little better to do than place ourselves in the hands of our all loving and all powerful God, who longs to shape us into the leaders he needs us to be in order to serve his kingdom purposes.

Go on. Stop for a day. Who knows what may come of it…

 Reflect

When and how do you stop, pause, and reflect? What is your rhythm for doing this on a daily, weekly, monthly, yearly basis? When you do stop, what are the things that help you to look back and look forward well? Who around you seems to do this and what could you learn from them?

Explore

- Use the Examen as a basis for reflection, www.ignatianspirituality.com/ignatian-prayer/the-examen

- Here are some suggestions for an annual review. Looking back: reflect on the blessings from God of this past year in your personal life, your work, your wider family. What was the greatest trial or difficulty of the past year? What have you learned from it? Looking forward: what is God seeking to teach you now? What are you praying for those closest to you? What is the priority in the year ahead in your personal development, your leadership, your relationships? Who do you long to see come to faith in Christ this year? What could you do to help that take place?

- For a longer process of reflection www.sharpeningleaders.com/to-the-point/60-minutes-of-year-end-reflection-3/

- You can download the Methodist covenant prayer along with a brief study guide www.rootsontheweb.com/content/PDFs/346041/Methodist_Covenant_Prayer_study.pdf

23. BALANCE VERSUS BLEND

⚙ Engage

We're often encouraged to get a more balanced life. Magazine articles provide surveys to help us find out how balanced our life is; personal management gurus encourage us to re-think our work–life balance. It all sounds so sensible, until you stop and think for a moment.

I am no longer convinced it is a helpful way to think about life. It suggests that work is somehow not part of life, and that it is possible to compartmentalize work (increasingly difficult in our digital age). It also suggests that there are just two things to get in balance, when in reality life is so much more complicated. It also has a whiff of blandness about it. Most leaders who achieve things aren't necessarily very balanced; they tend to be rather focused.

In our work with leaders we shifted to talking about blend rather than balance. The phrase we use to capture it is: our aim is to glorify God through a surrendered life that leads to an abundant life lived out in a blended life. The blended life is one where we recognize the centrality of God, Father, Son, and Holy Spirit, in our lives. He is Lord of all, of every aspect of our lives, and we surrender ourselves to him so that we might glorify his name with the whole of our lives.

Our relationship with him permeates every aspect of our lives, of which there are many. For example, I am a husband, father to three children, son to one living parent, sibling to my brothers and sisters, neighbour, friend, godparent. I also have a job, am part of a community, a global citizen, enjoy sport, and have a variety of interests and hobbies. I used to think of work as God's call and the rest of life as somehow separate. I now see all of this as part of God's call on my life and my discipleship is to work out how to live my one life in a way which honours God's call in every area of it. This involves blending and re-blending.

Just like everyone else, I have twenty-four hours in a day, and seven days in a week, so prayerfully discerning priorities is part of how I decide the appropriate blend for this season in my life. When we had three children under five there was no time for hobbies. When my father was very ill with dementia there was less time for work. As one section expands another by necessity must contract.

In all of this we seek to blend in a way that glorifies God and reflects the priorities of the kingdom. That means sacrifice and cost are part of the blend, and endurance and perseverance are necessary.

Part of taking stock as leaders is to set time aside to reflect on our blend so we may give ourselves wholeheartedly to whatever we are doing, be that in the home, at work, or within the community, and through this to bring glory to God.

 ## Reflect

---

What is your current blend? How does this reflect God's call on your life and the priorities in your life? What would an appropriate re-blend look like for this season of your life? When will you next rethink your blend?

 ## Explore

---

- *Insight into Stress*, Bev Shepherd (CWR). Shepherd explores the relationship between stress and pressure from a Christian perspective, with lots of practical suggestions on handling stress well.

- Create a visual image of your current blend. On a large piece of paper write God at the centre and place a light dotted oval around him. Now draw a large oval filling the rest of the page. This oval represents your life – twenty-four hours a day, seven days a week, fifty-two weeks a year. You can't expand the oval; you can reorder the blend of things in it. Begin to place aspects of God's call on your life in broad categories in this bigger oval (such as work role, spouse, friend) with a dotted line between each. Eventually you will end up with an oval with different "segments". Reflect on the size of those segments in this season of your life. What may need to expand or contract? What is an appropriate God-honouring blend?

24. BOUNDARIES

⚙ Engage

It's a constant debate. I heard it again last week. An older leader asks me why a recently ordained younger person is so fixed in only being prepared to work "two sessions" of the day. A business person reflects on the Gen Y graduates who enter her workplace and their sense of entitlement to boundaries that mean they won't be available outside their contracted hours.

It is also a constant struggle. Anyone in leadership, especially in leadership in the "caring" professions, knows how hard it is to work out appropriate boundaries.

I am reading two books at the moment on "pastoral ministry", both of them trying to navigate around this tricky situation of what are appropriate boundaries for a leader in church life, both honestly admitting they have got it wrong on more than one occasion.

When teaching about this on the Arrow Leadership Programme we talk about a continuum of boundary keeping, from fixed to fluid. There are those at the fixed end who are never prepared to move a boundary. A church leader won't attend anything on their day-off, no matter how much notice they are given to change the day; or they won't allow anyone into the vicarage or manse because they have decided to protect it as "home", and they don't want work to impinge on home. The school teacher who won't ever work into the evening on a Tuesday night because that is his "date night". The distribution manager who never goes into the distribution centre on the weekend because she is contracted to work weekdays.

There are those at the fluid end for whom boundaries hardly exist. The minister who responds to interruptions when preparing a sermon even if that means, yet again, a late Saturday night finishing off the preparation eating into family time. The home group leader who listens to an individual's ongoing crisis at the end the meeting knowing they have a teenager at home who needs help with their homework for tomorrow. The business person whose smart phone buzzes late into the evening, constantly drawing attention away from a night with friends as she responds to its insistent note.

It seems to me neither is a great place to be: so fixed that we miss real need or opportunity, so fluid that we wear ourselves out or begin to succumb to the lie of our "indispensability".

I think there may be a smaller continuum within the bigger one – firm to flexible. This is where we have a clear idea of some firm boundaries; health giving boundaries that enable us to keep leading for the long haul. Yet also flexible, where we are open to the unexpected, the opportunity, the need. Jesus seemed to be able to reside in this place as he left early in the morning to pray (firm, Mark 1:35) and also interrupted his journey to attend to the need (flexible) of a single voice crying out from the crowd (Mark 10:46–52).

What might these boundaries look like for us? It will depend on our personality, role, context, stage of life, and season of circumstance. Wisdom will know when to be more firm or more flexible. But as leaders it helps to think carefully about our boundaries, and to pray for God's wisdom to use them well.

 Reflect

Where are you currently on the boundary spectrum from fixed through firm to flexible to fluid? Reflect on why you are there. Identify where you would like to be in this season of your life and how you could move to that place.

⊕ Explore

- *Boundaries*, Henry Cloud (Zondervan). The classic text on boundaries, and there are a variety of related books including *Boundaries for Leaders*.

- You can also listen to Cloud speaking about leadership and boundaries at www.youtube.com/watch?v=d37CfbJjOkU

- Ask both those you lead and those in your personal relational context to give you some feedback on how they think you engage with boundaries. You may like to invite them to read this reflection in order to give them the spectrum as a way of thinking about your approach to boundaries. Don't be defensive, simply listen and receive their comments and then reflect on what you can learn from them.

25. LEADERSHIP IS HARD

⚙ Engage

In my conversations with leaders it is not unusual for someone to speak about going through some struggles related to their leadership role. This might be at the level of frustration with the structures of the wider organization or church, or struggles in relating to a colleague, or discouragement at something that seemed to be going so well but has now fallen apart.

These things are not deal breakers, but just the ongoing normal realities of leadership, the things that stretch us, discourage us, and, on occasions, make us wonder why we bother.

In her excellent book *Unleashing the Power of Rubber Bands*, Nancy Ortberg describes a talk she gave entitled "Stop being surprised that leadership is hard". Whilst the title may not win any points on the pastoral sensitivity front, the content is strangely liberating as she outlines why leadership is so hard (buy the book to find out).

Her point is simple: "Leadership is hard, and we all need to stop being surprised by that. We need to give it a slight chuckle and a nod, and keep going."

When leadership is a struggle it helps to have someone to talk to (friend, colleague, mentor), it helps to pray honestly (thoughts and feelings), and it helps to maintain a life blend that means work isn't all we do.

But it can also help to keep some perspective, to remember struggles are a part of leadership, and that by God's grace they can also be the times of personal growth.

So next time you hear me talking about my struggles as a leader, please offer me a listening ear, encourage me to pray and to practice living out 1 Thessalonians 5:16–18, but also remind me it goes with the territory, and urge me to keep going through the struggles. I will try and do the same for you.

For as Paul reminds those in church leadership in Colossians 1:24–2:3, we struggle that those we serve may be presented mature in Christ. That is worth the struggle.

 Reflect

What does struggle look like for you in your leadership role at this time? In what ways can you minimize the struggle? In what ways can you get used to the reality that "leadership is hard"?

⊕ Explore

* *Unleashing the Power of Rubber Bands*, Nancy Ortberg (Tyndale). It covers a great range of leadership topics in an accessible style.

* *Facing Disappointment*, James Newcome (Grove Leadership Series No. 25). A searingly honest account of disappointment in the life of a senior leader and how to handle it well.

HOW NOT TO LOSE HEART

GRAHAM ARCHER

Twice in 2 Corinthians 4 Paul writes "we do not lose heart". In the surrounding chapters, he not only gives us some practical tips about how to do this, he also explains why it is something of a miracle that he remains in good heart. From this second letter to the church in Corinth, there is no doubt that his work of leadership has been very tough indeed. There are lists of his sufferings and pressures, but these verses illustrate it most clearly to me.

> *We do not want you to be uninformed, brothers and*
> *sisters, about the troubles we experienced in the province of*
> *Asia. We were under great pressure, far beyond our ability*
> *to endure, so that we despaired of life itself. Indeed, we felt*
> *we had received the sentence of death.*
>
> **2 Corinthians 1:8–9**

No one would argue with Paul's "right" to be downhearted, yet somehow amid the stonings, beatings, anxiety, and sleeplessness he managed to "not lose heart".

Proverbs 4:23 holds the iconic exhortation "Above all else, guard your heart, for everything you do flows from it". Let's see if we can pick up some tips from Paul in 2 Corinthians that help us do just that as Christian leaders.

KNOWING OUR DEPENDENCY

"This happened that we might not rely on ourselves but on God, who raises the dead" (1:9); "On him we have set our hope" (1:10). This is strong language – Paul isn't just saying that a product of tough times is the benefit of resilience; he seems to be implying that God allowed the suffering in order to toughen him up. Elsewhere he speaks of suffering leading to endurance and hope, and in these chapters develops the thought stream that unjust, unexpected, and uncomfortable times can produce a profound reliance on God if we let them.

Christian leaders need this. What use is a leader who believes that he or she can do God's work with their own wisdom and resources alone (and maybe for their own glory)? We could choose to rely on him right now even if life isn't tough: to move in our prayers to expressing utter dependency and relinquishing self-sufficiency. Despite his learning, Paul claims no competency of his own, it is all from God (3:4–6).

NEVER WALK ALONE

Much of this opening section is written in the "we" form. "We were under pressure… we speak… we are very bold… we do not distort… we have this treasure… we do not lose heart." In contrast, chapter two verse twelve is in the "I" form. "The Lord had opened a door for me" to preach the gospel in Troas; but he then goes on to say that as he had lost track of Titus, so he moved on instead to Macedonia to look for him. Can this be right? God gave him an opportunity for ministry and he didn't take it because his partner was missing and didn't want to go it alone? Examples of followers of Jesus being commissioned to solo ministry are fairly rare in the New Testament, so why might we think that leadership can be a solitary exercise? Are there areas of leadership where we are solo, separate, independent, lonely, even, and vulnerable to unhealthy isolation? Might we pause in our leadership long enough to seek out our own Titus, Barnabas, Dave, or Eileen?

DON'T LOOK DOWN

Despite being a sinner, he has a healthy sense of his own eternal glory. There is nothing in these chapters that belittles his calling. According to chapter three his ministry is glorious. The ministry of the old Jewish covenant written on stones was pretty glorious, but this one, written on human hearts, is out of this world.

Our humanness can tempt us to see our leadership calling in a much less glorious light. "My leadership isn't appreciated by my boss…", "My church is rather small…", "I am only a very part-time leader…", "I'm not as successful as…", "People don't really notice what I do…". These reference points have very little place in Paul's language. He is by grace a competent minister of a life-giving gospel who is gradually being transformed into the likeness of Jesus with an ever increasing capacity to reflect God's unsurpassed and unfading glory. And none of that has to do with his status, success or pride; it is all about God's grace. So when we are tempted to be down on our efforts or minimize our potential, let's remind ourselves of just how big our calling is and allow ourselves the encouragement of chapter three verse twelve: "Therefore, since we have such a hope we are very bold."

MORE THAN SKIN DEEP

Paul understands the difference between his inner and outer life. His reference to faces reflecting the Lord's glory has nothing to do with a Hollywood smile or whether we moisturize. His thesis goes more than skin deep. Our bodies are jars of clay (chapter 4) or earthly tents (chapter 5) and both images are subject to the normal laws of decay. But the treasure in the jar is not and neither is the eternal tent that the treasure will one day inhabit.

In our image-obsessed world with its endless quest for the secret of eternal youth, Paul's straight talking is quite refreshing. "Outwardly we are wasting away YET inward we are being renewed day by day" (4:16). Leaders should attend to their appearance. We communicate by more than just words, so our body language, demeanour, vitality or weariness, clothes, and general health have the potential to help or hinder the message. These things matter, but they are not our defining feature. Paul presumably had scars from his beatings, tendonitis from the manacles, maybe a limp, possibly a speech impediment, and most certainly bags under his eyes; but those eyes were fixed on that which is unseen and eternal and that was his ultimate definition (4:18). Of his own hardships he wrote these "light and momentary troubles are achieving for us an eternal glory that far outweighs them all" (4:17).

IN CONCLUSION

Maybe today is a day when you feel like giving up – you've lost heart, or maybe you have been there for some time. As you take that into prayer verbalize your dependency again on God to restore you, search out a trusted friend for support, remind yourself that living for him is still a high and noble calling, and allow God to carry you through.

Graham is Director of Ministry at CPAS, having been a missionary in Japan, a church planter, and leader of a larger church. He is author of Don't Lose Heart *(Grove Leadership Series No. 16).*

ACTION REVIEW

THE INNER LIFE – ESTABLISHING RHYTHMS

Reflect on section 5 using the questions below. Identify one thing you are going to do in response to what God has been prompting in you as a result of your stocktake so far. Remember, it is best to keep it as a simple and doable action.

What action are you going to take?

When and how are you going to take this action?

Who are you going to share this action with for support and accountability?

How will you incorporate this action into your prayer life?

REFLECTIONS

REFLECTIONS

REFLECTIONS

SECTION
6

THE OUTER LIFE – PRESSING AHEAD

Your best leadership efforts are needed on a daily basis, right where you are.

Nancy Ortberg

A LEADERSHIP PRAYER

Lord, thank you for your call on my life to lead.
The arms of God be around my shoulders,
The touch of the Holy Spirit be upon my head,
The sign of Christ's cross be upon my forehead,
The sound of the Holy Spirit in my ears,
The fragrance of the Holy Spirit in my nostrils,
The vision of heaven's company in my eyes,
The conversation of heaven's company on my lips,
The work of God's Church in my hands,
The service of God and neighbour in my feet,
A home for God in my heart,
And to God, the Father of all, my entire being.
Amen.

St Fursey (adapted)

26. RHETORIC VERSUS REALITY

⚙ Engage

There is a tension in leadership. The tension between what we say about things and the reality of how things are. I come across this tension all the time.

The senior management team talk about the way the new system is changing the culture of the organization; the employees talk about how the system is fragmenting the organization. The diocese speaks positively of a new scheme they are implementing; the clergy in the parishes speak negatively of the same scheme. The minister of a church speaks of things in glowing terms at the Church Meeting; the people in the pews speak of things in hushed tones at the end of the meeting.

The higher up you go, or the longer you are in a leadership role, the more difficult it is to hear the reality.

It would be easy to dismiss the rhetoric and focus on the reality, but this is too simplistic a solution. Part of leadership *is* helping people to see a different future, raising people's eyes to possibilities, encouraging people to move from where things are now to where things might be. The old Anglo-Saxon word for leader reminds us that it is about a route, or path; it is about going somewhere. The danger is that those at the centre believe the rhetoric is the current reality, or lose touch with the reality on the ground. If the rhetoric doesn't connect with the reality it stays just that, rhetoric.

Therefore, as leaders we need to work hard at getting feedback, listening carefully to what is being said on the ground, and acknowledging reality in every way we can. This involves setting up processes by which people can say things to us, everything from a questionnaire to a surgery slot to a feedback loop built into every meeting.

We also need to have around us people who will speak truth kindly to us, so that we don't isolate ourselves from the harder things we would rather not hear; people who will let us know what others are saying and thinking.

Then when we speak of what might be, it will be connected with what is. And when we speak of what is, it will be connected with what might be. For leadership involves both clarifying and communicating the rhetoric at the centre, and engaging well with the reality on the ground.

 Reflect

----

What are your "feedback loops" at the moment? Who will speak "reality" to you? How can you encourage both of these? What are your natural tendencies when receiving feedback? Which ones may you need to be careful to monitor?

Explore

One of the critical things for development as a leader is helpful feedback. Yet, it isn't always easy to give or receive. Take a look at the following for helpful ideas and insights.

- *Thanks for the Feedback*, Douglas Stone and Sheila Heen (Penguin). Here the authors speak about the main themes at a gathering of Google staff. www.youtube.com/watch?v=SggjK0Gm3I4 and you can also read their article for the Harvard Business review on finding the coach in criticism https://hbr.org/2014/01/find-the-coaching-in-criticism

- Ian Paul writes on how to give and receive feedback www.psephizo.com /life-ministry/how-to-give-and-receive-feedback-2/

27. GROWING LEADERS

⚙ Engage

Recently I gave a talk on developing others as leaders. At the end a thoughtful church leader asked a great question that got me thinking.

In the talk I outlined three stages in developing others as leaders taken from Mark 3:13–19 through to Mark 6.

- **Discern who** – best done in prayer and in consultation with others.

- **Develop** – best done by inviting people to be "with you" as Jesus did, because so much of leadership is caught as much as taught.

- **Deploy** – best done by giving people appropriate responsibilities because it is as people have a go at leading that they learn to lead.

I also mentioned the *Growing Leaders* suite of resources CPAS has that provides materials to use in developing leaders over an eight to twelve month period. Then came the question.

"We don't have the resources or inclination as yet to commit to a course like *Growing Leaders*, what can I do in the meantime to help those leaders we have to grow?" Good question. Here are a few ideas:

- Identify those who are in leadership roles and invite them to a session where you provide some input on leadership and give space for conversation and reflection. The input could be from you directly, someone else in your context, or watching a talk someone else has given. Alternatively interview someone in a significant leadership role about their life and leadership and explore both what they have learnt about leadership and how their faith interacts with their leadership responsibility. Do this once a term over a year and it will be a huge help to those who attend.

- Create a book group where you gather a few leaders who commit to read a leadership book a chapter at a time, and then meet to discuss the chapter once a month (you could start with the *Growing Leaders* book).

- Invite people into leadership triplets for a specific length of time (three months?) where they meet once a week or fortnight for forty-five minutes to talk about the leadership roles in their lives and pray for one another.

- Create a library of resources that people could borrow (books, articles, DVDs, magazines) and promote it among your leaders. You could start with some of the resources mentioned in this book.

- Use the LICC idea of *This Time Tomorrow* to interview and pray for a leader in your Sunday gathering over a whole term. For more on *This Time Tomorrow* see www.licc.org.uk/resources/this-time-tomorrow/

Anything that helps develop others as leaders is a good thing, and just as perhaps others have invested in us, let us invest in those we are called to serve.

Reflect

Who are you investing in to develop as leaders (please think all ages not just adult)? What would be the best way to invest in them over the coming year?

 Explore

- Create a people chain out of paper. Write on each the name of one person you would like to see develop in your context as a leader. Be sure to think all ages (young people as well the retired), both genders, and those who may be thought of as an unlikely prospect. Then work out (preferably with others) what next step would help them to develop as a leader, and prayerfully action that next step.

- The *Growing Leaders* suite of resources includes a ten session course for adults, an eight session course for teenagers, and three books: *Growing Leaders*, James Lawrence (BRF); *Growing Young Leaders*, Ruth Hassall (BRF); *Ready to Lead*, Ruth Hassall (BRF). For more information, see www.cpas.org.uk/growingleaders

- *Growing Leaders from Diverse Cultures: Leadership in a Multicultural Church*, Andy Jolley (Grove Leadership Series No. 21). Jolley shares insights from working in inner city Birmingham for many years.

- Ian Paul's blog, subtitled "scholarship. serving. ministry.", covers a wide variety of topics relevant to those in leadership and offers a breadth of scholarship that is both stimulating and provocative: www.psephizo.com

28. OPEN DOORS

 **Engage**

Jonah is an intriguing book. The first three verses set up the scenario the rest of the book explores.

> *The word of the Lord came to Jonah son of Amittai:*
> *"Go to the great city of Nineveh and preach against it,*
> *because its wickedness has come before me." But Jonah ran*
> *away from the Lord and headed for Tarshish.*

In his book, *All the Places to Go*, John Ortberg suggests that most of us have open doors God is inviting us to walk through. Some are big; a call to Nineveh would fit into this category, as would a call to stand up for justice within our community, or a call to take on a significant leadership role.

Some are (relatively) small; a slightly tricky conversation, getting out of bed to pray, or daring to say something about the good news of Jesus in a conversation with those who aren't yet followers of Christ.

As we face these open doors we have a decision to make. Do we walk towards them, or flee in the opposite direction? Ortberg goes on to identify a range of factors that led Jonah to choose the latter.

As a leader there are nearly always open doors before me. I can identify two at the moment that if I am honest weigh on my mind. When we face such doors, perhaps it will help us to reflect on the following questions:

- What is preventing me from pressing forward?

- What temptation is enticing me away from this door towards another?

- What would the consequences be of walking through the door? Of not walking through the door?

- Who can I talk this through with?

Part of the leader's role is to spot and push on doors, some of them clearly open, others only ajar. We also encourage others to do the same. Thankfully Jonah teaches us that even when we have failed to do this, God is still faithful, he will fulfil his purposes, but how much better to cooperate with God in the first place than flee in another direction.

 **Reflect**

Which door do you stand before at the moment? What is written on the door? What would it take to walk on through?

 **Explore**

- *All The Places to Go*, John Ortberg (Tyndale)

- A fascinating TED talk on the power of the body to influence how we approach some open doors, like interviews, tricky conversations, and tough situations. How might this help us in our leadership? www.ted.com/talks/amy_cuddy_your_body_language_shapes_ who_you_are

29. FIRE BULLETS, THEN CANNON BALLS

⚙ **Engage**

There are times when we have the opportunity to start something new as a leader, or to do something in a different way. Perhaps it is the start of a new year, a new term, or a new season. New possibilities, new ideas, new openings. But which one to go for?

On behalf of those they lead, leaders spend time thinking about where things have come from, how things are at the moment, and where things might be going. Leaders take stock of an organization, a department, a small group, a club, or a church. In the process we may identify a range of creative possibilities, but how do we decide where to invest time, energy, and money?

In one of his excellent books, *Great by Choice*, Jim Collins suggests "fire bullets, not cannon balls". The analogy is simple. Imagine a Tudor warship with an enemy ship bearing down on it. It has just enough gunpowder left for two cannon ball shots. If it pours it all into the cannon, shoots, misses by 40 metres, then fires another shot and misses by 5 metres, they're sunk. Literally!

However, if it takes a little of the gunpowder and fires several bullets until it gets the right trajectory, and then uses the remaining to fire the cannon ball on target, it may survive the battle for another day.

So with new possibilities ahead, new ideas to try, fire a few bullets before you pour all your energy into the project. In CPAS we call them pilots (in the business world they are also called parallel runs, dress rehearsal testing, proof of concepts, or user acceptance testing). We pilot a lot of things. Some work out, some don't. But when we discover one that works really well, we are then able to go for it big time.

Good pilots often involve some risk taking, but by calling them pilots (or trials) people are normally prepared to give them a go knowing that they are not embarking on something that will be established forever: we're just "giving it a go". Pilots also allow for review and learning, so the final version is better than the initial.

In this way, firing bullets then cannon balls can lead to more regular hitting of the target, more people being on board with the project, and a better quality product. It also means we will be wise stewards of precious resources, investing well for the sake of the kingdom. Over the years many wonderful, life transforming initiatives have started with a few carefully aimed shots, which have then led to bigger things happening than anyone could have imagined.

 **Reflect**

What project are you thinking about initiating? What would a pilot look like? When and how would you get it started with a few carefully targeted shots?

 **Explore**

- *Great by Choice*, Jim Collins (Random House)

- Asking good questions is a key leadership skill, and when starting a new initiative the right questions will open things up and clarify the way ahead. *Great Questions for Leading Well* brings together a wide variety of helpful questions to ask www.arrowleadership.org/great-questions-for-leading-well/

30. CONVERSATIONS

 **Engage**

----

*At its core, we speak the truth in love when we care enough
to speak the gospel into the lives of those around us. This
is God's everyday calling for every Christian.*

Tony Reinke

Leaders spend a lot of time talking with people – formally and informally,
in one-to-one settings, and in meetings of many people.

Some of the conversations will be catching up with what happened
yesterday or asking how someone is. These are important. They establish
relationship and show we care. Leaders who can't engage in "small-talk"
can appear distant or stand-offish.

There is another type of conversation though. It is intentional,
focused, and enables people or things to move forward. We see Jesus
having these conversations with those he meets with startling results: for
example the woman at the well (John 4:1–26) or Peter (John 21:15–23).

Here are three categories of intentional conversations that I find it
helpful to have:

- **Encouraging conversations** – a few well-chosen words can build
  someone up. Yet my tendency is sometimes to think encouraging
  things but not say them. For example, in a meeting yesterday I was
  thinking what good questions someone was asking, but that is not
  enough. I had to intentionally say: "It's great to work with you on
  this. You always bring such good questions to the issues that really
  help us explore things from a different perspective." I could sense
  them stand a little taller.

- **Developmental conversations** – someone comes to you asking for you to make a decision about something. It is far quicker and easier to make the decision and move on to something else. But that doesn't develop the person. It may take more time to ask "What are your thoughts on this?", explore other options with them, ask some pertinent questions, and then say "I'd be really happy with either of those options, why don't you decide", but it will help the person grow in their confidence in decision making.

- **Tricky conversations** – we all know these. The ones we'd rather avoid. They often fall to a leader because no one else wants to have them, and because it is part of our role. Poor behaviour that needs to be addressed, an attitude that could do with toning down, a broken relationship that could do with some attention. Tricky, but necessary. One leader speaks of daring to enter the "tunnel of chaos". I constantly need to remind myself to not walk away from such conversations.

I wonder which conversation God might be prompting you to have this week?

☀ Reflect

Which of these three types of intentional conversations do you find it easier to have, and which do you find harder to have? Why? Think about three people you lead with – is there an intentional conversation it would be good to have with each of them?

🕐 Explore

- *Crucial Conversations*, Patterson, Grenny, McMillan, Switzler (McGraw Hill). You can see one of the authors, Joseph Grenny, speaking on crucial conversations at www.youtube.com/watch?v=-dKYunkN0Bs

- *Transforming Conversation: How Jesus Talked to People*, Rob Bewley (Grove Biblical Series No. 61)

31. BONUS DAY – MEETINGS MATTER

⚙ Engage

We've unearthed some scary stats. Really. You may need to sit down. Ready?

The average church leader has 564 meetings a year. That is 846 hours a year, the equivalent of 105 working days. I imagine the figures aren't much different for those who lead in other spheres.

Or how about this one?

In the Anglican Church in England a staggering 125,000 people spend around 1,500,000 hours a year attending PCC meetings. That is the equivalent of 513 years of working days every year.

Phew!

Meetings. Love them or hate them, leaders have a lot of them. Everything from the informal coffee with someone to chat about their next job, through to the more formal gathering of the volunteer youth leaders to dream up the programme for next term.

To be honest, I used to resent most of the meetings I attended. I saw them as a hindrance to the real work of "ministry". That was until a wiser and more mature leader said to me: "James, meetings are ministry. Learn to love them, and make each one you attend the best it can possibly be."

I've learnt a lot over the years, both from reading and observing. Here are three out of many things that can help meetings go well:

- **Tip 1: Be clear about purpose** – why are we having this meeting? Good meetings are time savers not time wasters. To help a meeting be good, be clear why it is happening, set the context for the conversation. At the more formal end of the spectrum, ensure that items discussed are worthy of being on the agenda by being *complex* enough and *weighty* enough to warrant people spending time thinking about them. If there isn't a sufficient reason for meeting, don't. At the more informal end of the spectrum, we probably won't have a set agenda, but we can still be clear about why we are meeting. Clarity of purpose produces energy in a meeting.

- **Tip 2: Prepare properly** – over the last eight years I've been in many meetings with a colleague of mine. He is always prepared for a meeting. Always. He's given it some thought, had a few ideas about the best process for what we are trying to achieve, has got some ideas to contribute to the conversation, and comes with clarity about why we are meeting. Not only is this impressive, it is a blessing. I have never been in a meeting with this person and left thinking "what a waste of time". Not once. It may be three minutes thought before a conversation, or two or three hours hard work leading into a major gathering, but one of the ways we value people is to prepare for meetings.

- **Tip 3: Seek to bless others** – if you have responsibility for the meeting, create a good environment by giving attention to the layout. Make decisions in a way that engages different personality types. Create a safe place for the timid to speak. Provide wonderful refreshments. Encourage healthy conflict. Be clear about actions. All these things (and many others) will help people to leave feeling energized, having had fun, and with a sense of contributing to something significant.

Meetings matter. If meetings we attend are boring, dysfunctional, or ineffective, as leaders we can do something about it. We have the privilege of shaping meetings to be fun, focused, and fruitful.

 Reflect

- -

Which one meeting you are responsible for could you most immediately improve? How? When?

 **Explore**

- *Death by Meetings*, Patrick Lencioni (John Wiley and Sons). Lencioni tells one of his classic leadership fables and then draws from it great ideas on what makes meetings go well.

- *PCC Tonight*, James Lawrence (CPAS)

- Leaders often spend lots of time in groups, and understanding group dynamics, how they work, and what to do if they aren't working well, is well worth thinking through. This is a helpful article that introduces useful concepts in group dynamics with practical ideas about how to handle common issues: www.mindtools.com/pages/article/improving-group-dynamics.htm

THE ART OF ASKING GOOD QUESTIONS

EMMA INESON

QUESTIONS ARE IMPORTANT

If I had an hour to solve a problem, and my life depended on the solution, I would spend the first fifty-five minutes determining the proper question to ask, for once I know the proper question, I could solve the problem in less than five minutes

Albert Einstein

It is easy to think that leadership is about having all the right answers, but I am becoming increasingly convinced that one of the tools of great leadership is knowing how to ask the right questions.

We know instinctively that questions are important. It's how we learn anything. One of the first things a child does is learn to ask questions. It's reported that a four-year-old asks 437 questions a day. But it seems that, as we grow older, we tend to grow out of the habit.

Think how many inventions have come about from someone asking the right question in the right place at the right time. Einstein's theory of relativity resulted from a question that he'd pondered since a teenager: "What would the universe look like if I were riding on the end of a light beam at the speed of light?" Consider also how many disasters might have been averted if someone had asked the right question. It is said that engineers who had concerns about the design of the Titanic didn't want to appear stupid by asking questions that didn't seem to bother the "experts".

THE BIBLE IS FULL OF QUESTIONS

Amongst God's first words to humans was a question, a multi-layered one: "Where are you?" (Genesis 3:9). The question leads Adam and Eve to confess not just where they are but what they've done. God seems to pose a lot of questions. He asks Job a series of questions which ultimately lead Job to greater understanding; "I will question you, and you declare to me. Will you even put me in the wrong? Will you condemn me that you may be justified? Have you an arm like God, and can you thunder with a voice like his?" (Job 40:7–9, RSV).

One of the first things we hear about Jesus is that he was, "in the temple courts, sitting among the teachers, listening to them and asking them questions" (Luke 2:46). Why did he need to ask them questions? He was God wasn't he? Shouldn't he just have sat there and told them all the answers? They were indeed amazed at his answers, but he seemed to think asking them questions was important too.

Jesus asked lots of questions. Someone has counted up 307 questions asked by Jesus. Many of his questions are rhetorical and lead the person he's talking to think further, to ask more questions, and to enter into a dialogue with him. We tend to focus on Jesus' clear propositional statements, and pay less attention to the questions he asked. But this could be to miss something very important. Richard Rohr writes: "… we have paid so little attention to Jesus' questions and emphasized instead his seeming answers. They give us more a feeling of success and closure. We have made of Jesus a systematic theologian, who walked around teaching dogmas, instead of a peripatetic and engaging transformer of the soul".

An example comes in Matthew 19, when the rich young ruler came to Jesus and asked, "Teacher, what good deed must I do to have eternal life?" (RSV). Instead of answering immediately, Jesus asks him a question back: "Why do you ask me about what is good?", challenging the man about who he thinks he is speaking to, "If only God is good, why do you call me good? Are you saying I am God? If so, why are you questioning me?" They go on to engage in an exchange in which both of them give answers and ask questions. Watching this causes the disciples to ask even more questions: "Then who can be saved?"

CONSTRUCTING GOOD QUESTIONS

So if questions were an important tool used by Jesus to lead people to new places, how might we harness the power of questioning in our leadership? Can we discern what is the right question to ask at the right time?

Good questions can do really useful work in discerning vision, in strategic planning, in chairing good meetings, in leading small groups, in mentoring, in coaching, and in pastoral relationships. But constructing the right question for the different contexts of leadership is an art, and a science – and takes deliberate thought and practice.

Firstly, it's worth thinking carefully about the **construction of a question**. The main thing to notice is that there are open and closed questions. Closed questions potentially stop the enquiry dead in its tracks, "Are you satisfied with our working relationship?" (yes/no). Open questions, on the other hand, have the potential to do something much more powerful.

In 1956 Benjamin Bloom created a system for categorising levels of questions in educational settings. Bloom's taxonomy ranks questions according to their power. The most basic questions are simply to do with ascertaining facts (remembering), but they progress through a scale from the least to the most powerful: understanding, applying, analyzing, evaluating, and finally, creating.

So, for example:

- "When have you been most satisfied with our working relationship?" (remembering).

- "What is it about our working relationship that you find most satisfying?" (analyzing).

- "Why might it be that our working relationship has had its ups and downs?" (evaluating).

- "What would a better working relationship look like?" (creating).

A powerful "creating" question is one that opens doors to new and fruitful possibilities and might include questions like, "If you had access to all resources how would you deal with...?", "How many ways can you...?", "What would happen if...?", "How else would you...?" The higher order questions are more powerful and open up more creative avenues. They do more.

Secondly, we need to consider the **scope of a question** – too wide and it will be useless, too narrow and it won't do the work we need it to do. Consider; "How can we change our home group?", "How can we change our local church?", "How can we change our diocese?", "How can we change the Church of England?" Tailor and clarify the scope as precisely as possible to keep the question within realistic boundaries and pertinent to the needs of the situation you are working with. Avoid stretching the scope of your question too far. The scope must be appropriate.

Finally, it's worth checking the **assumptions contained in a question**. They might betray a hidden agenda that stops the question doing its truly open work. Consider; "What went wrong and who is responsible?", compared with, "What can we learn from what's happened and what potential options do we now see?"

Some large German companies place such a high value on powerful questions that they actually employ a "Direktor Grundsatzfragen" (Director of Fundamental Questions). I wonder if, as leaders, we might become the Direktor Grundsatzfragen for our organizations, churches, and communities, encouraging a "culture of enquiry" and using good questions to lead us to new places and to open up new possibilities.

This article is based on some work by Vogt, Brown, and Isaacs. See Vogt, E., Brown, J., and Isaacs, D. 2003, *The Art of Powerful Questions: Catalysing Insight, Innovation and Action* (Whole Systems Associates).

Emma is Principal of Trinity College Bristol, a Church of England theological college, member of General Synod, and author of several books.

BONUS ARTICLE: LEADING AS A SINGLE PERSON

KATE WHARTON

A while ago I wrote a book entitled *Single Minded*. I hope that it's a useful resource – for single people seeking to live life to the full, for married people seeking to better understand and support their single friends, and for leaders seeking to make their churches places of welcome for single people.

Since I wrote the book, and as I speak about singleness, people often want to discuss with me what it's like to lead as a single person. Clearly, it's the only sort of leadership I've ever known. I've done a lot of thinking about it, and was delighted to write this article.

So what is it like to lead as a single person? If you're married, and perhaps especially if you've been married for longer than you've been a leader, you might be wondering what difference it makes – surely leading is leading, whatever your life circumstances? If you're a single leader, though, you've probably already thought of ten issues.

I'm going to explore some of the things that I think are particularly pertinent to single people in church leadership. In some cases they are, of course, also things which affect married people – but perhaps affect single people more or differently. Some of these things would apply to those leading outside a church context too.

LONELINESS

The thing which comes immediately to mind when I think about leading as a single person is loneliness. I guess leadership always feel a bit lonely, as it requires making many decisions, some of which may be difficult and unpopular. If you're a leader who isn't single, then you might wonder why I've started here – you may also experience loneliness in leadership, so what's the difference?

I would say yes, sometimes leadership can be lonely whoever we are and whatever our life circumstances – but there is a difference for single people.

For me, the issue is that there isn't anyone there to talk to, or to process with, or to download to. If you're married, I realize it doesn't necessarily follow that you can discuss leadership issues with your spouse. But nevertheless, there is someone there. There's someone there in those few moments before you go off to do something big or scary, to see your anxiety and offer some comfort. There's someone there when you return from a difficult meeting or conversation, to allow you to unwind. There's someone there when life is stressful and busy, to make you a cup of tea or put the bins out or just sit and watch TV with.

I think perhaps the issue is this – leadership can be lonely, and living alone as a single person can be lonely, so if you put them together, that's a potentially difficult combination.

If you're a single leader who struggles with loneliness, I'd recommend you work out some things which will help you in those tough times – find some people to pray with regularly, find a mentor and/or spiritual director to talk to, know who the people are who you can call or text when you get in late at night and just need to tell someone about your day, find other ways to process, such as journaling, find people to have fun with.

EXPECTATIONS

Another thing which can be an issue for single leaders is other people's expectations, particularly in a church leadership context. (I know – this one's also an issue for married leaders too. But again, I think it's a bit different.)

As leaders, we all know only too well that other people can expect things of us which are simply impossible to fulfil. Sometimes it can feel as if everyone around us expects something different from us, and that Jesus himself would find it hard to meet all their expectations.

Married leaders will be familiar with the hope of some churches that their spouse will be an extra leader, so that they get "double their money" in terms of pastoral care or ministry. Sometimes the spouse wishes to function in such a leadership role, of course, but sometimes they don't.

What you might not realize if you're not single is that there are also a number of expectations placed on single leaders. Sometimes it seems that we're expected to do the work of an entire family, to be able to work 24/7 because we have no (family) reason not to, and to be always available. People quiz us constantly about our singleness – why on earth aren't we married with children?

And of course it's very easy to put unhelpful expectations onto ourselves and to work in ways which are unhelpful – to ask too much of ourselves, to not take enough time off, to work crazy hours, to not be accountable to anyone.

Something which I've found that people often don't realize if they're not single is just how much time is taken up with cooking, cleaning, shopping, gardening, and just general life admin. There's no one else to do those things so I somehow need to find the time to do all of them myself.

And then there's the time off side of things – if I'm going to see friends or family on my day off (which I really need to do if I'm going to stay sane), it might require more time and effort, planning in advance, and often having to drive some distance (which generally I do, as the one who's more flexible and able to travel).

COMMITMENT

But, enough of the negativity. There are some great things about being a single leader too. One of them I think is a flip side of what I've already mentioned. As a single leader I can totally commit myself to the congregation or group or ministry that I'm leading. Not in a negative "I have no life beyond" way, but in a positive "I am able to be totally present for you" way.

I really like the fact that I can rearrange my plans at a moment's notice, should I need to. I can invite people round without needing to check with anyone else, or drop everything to go and visit someone. I can use my house and garden and car as a means of hospitality and blessing, because no one besides me needs them. I can be flexible with my time, meeting people (where reasonable) at a time that suits them.

Paul puts it like this (in The Message version of 1 Corinthians 7:33–34): "Marriage involves you in all the nuts and bolts of domestic life and in wanting to please your spouse, leading to so many more demands on your attention. The time and energy that married people spend on caring for and nurturing each other, the unmarried can spend in becoming whole and holy instruments of God."

I don't want to suggest single people are more holy than married people, obviously! But I think there is a great bonus for single people in terms of the way they can order their time and energy because they are free of some of the commitments of married people.

PERSPECTIVE

My final thought on the plus side of being a single leader is that I can bring that viewpoint and perspective to everything that I do, including to quite a few places where it might not normally be heard. Ask most single Christians and they'll tell you that church can often feel like a very couply, family-orientated place. It's obviously right and proper that churches are welcoming to families – but unfortunately this sometimes means that singles feel left out. As a single leader I can be a role model to single Christians, and remind them that they aren't odd or unusual or unwelcome. I can bring a different perspective to things and maybe challenge some assumptions or norms.

I also wonder whether being a single leader enables me to have a voice, not just for other single people, but for anyone who doesn't quite "fit" into the normal way of things, for whatever reason. Our society and our Church still generally expect people to be in couples and so when you're not, people can treat you differently. Clearly that isn't the same as being treated differently for other reasons, but perhaps I can empathize a bit, and perhaps I can speak out and speak up for those who feel on the edge.

Kate Wharton is a vicar and Area Dean in Everton, and author of Single Minded *(Monarch).*

ACTION REVIEW

THE OUTER LIFE – PRESSING AHEAD

Reflect on section 6 using the questions below. Identify one thing you are going to do in response to what God has been prompting in you as a result of your stocktake so far. Remember, it is best to keep it as a simple and doable action.

What action are you going to take?

When and how are you going to take this action?

Who are you going to share this action with for support and accountability?

How will you incorporate this action into your prayer life?

REFLECTIONS

146

REFLECTIONS

TAKING STOCK – THE NEXT STEP

Using these thirty (or thirty-one) reflections, you've taken stock of some aspects of your leadership. As I mentioned at the start, there are many other themes we could have explored. My hope is that you have been able to identify some ways to grow and develop as a leader, and that you have found taking stock a helpful process.

Don't stop now.

I've been privileged over many years to work with some wonderful leaders. What has made them such good role models? Their engaging personality? No. Their academic ability? No. Their innate leadership skills? No. Their thick skin? No. Their wisdom? No.

The one thing all these leaders have shared has been a commitment to reflect on what they do and an openness to learn. They are great stocktakers. Year-on-year they grow in both the inner and outer life of their leadership.

Taking stock is ideally a part of our life rhythm, built into our diaries and reflected in our practices. I hope you will continue to use some of the tools provided in this book to continue a life-long commitment to ongoing stocktaking. And if the monthly Lead On email can be a help in that process, why not sign up today at www.cpas.org.uk/leadon.

ADDITIONAL AIDS FOR TAKING STOCK

I've included two further things to help with the process of taking stock. Both will need to be adapted to your particular circumstances, but hopefully can provide a starting point for thinking about either a quiet day or a sabbatical.

The first is a suggested outline for a quiet day (or part of a day). For those who aren't used to setting aside a day to think and pray it can be quite daunting to work out how to approach it. Ultimately it is best to work out what works for you, but the following may provide a place to start.

The second is some suggestions for those who are privileged to be able to take a sabbatical. These periods of extended leave can be a great help, but can also be tricky to plan and sometimes difficult to navigate.

TAKING A QUIET DAY

Beware of the work you do for God destroying the work he wants to do in you.

Bill Hybels

Taking time to be with God is a priority for any Christian leader. Sadly in the busyness of life and leadership it is so easy to allow this to be squeezed out. Time each day is vital, but many also find that practising the spiritual disciplines of stillness, solitude, and silence is a helpful way to maintain a vibrant relationship with Jesus.

Perhaps the easiest way to do this is to join an organized quiet day. Many Christian retreat centres around the country have a regular pattern of running such days, often themed.

But if you would rather be on your own, the following guidelines are offered in the hope they may provide some insights in how to make use of a day set aside to be with God. There are many ways of doing this, and many resources available to help. Some are listed at the end of this outline.

HOW OFTEN?

For most people establishing a regular pattern is a real help. This may be taking an evening or a day aside once a month, every six weeks, every two months, three times a year. Whatever, the key is to establish the pattern, put it in the diary, and stick to it. Be warned, everything will conspire against you taking this time.

WHERE TO GO?

It's important to find somewhere that helps you to relax and be still and quiet. A retreat house, a friend's home if they are not using it, a particular spot of natural beauty (although be aware that ideally you need a place you can go to in all seasons). It needs to be relatively nearby, because you don't want to spend lots of time travelling.

HOW LONG?

This will depend on your personal circumstances. Some find it really helpful to go the night before and that enables them to have a relaxing evening simply unwinding. Others go for the day i.e. 9 a.m. – 4 p.m. Whichever, I advise you make sure that you don't have anything work-oriented planned into your diary for the evening of that day, and preferably nothing major planned for the next day, otherwise you will spend your whole time with your mind on what you've got to do.

WHAT DO I FOCUS ON?

Be clear about the purpose of the time. I think a quiet day set aside to spend time with God is different from a prayer day. The latter is important, but normally involves us going with a set idea of what we want to do, i.e. to pray specifically for some aspect of our lives or leadership. Nor is it a study day where we take loads of books (albeit Christian ones) to learn more about God, or the work we're doing. The whole focus of a quiet day set aside to be with God is simply to meet with him, and in that sense we allow God to set the agenda. It is a day of abandoning ourselves into his hands. We are saying "Here I am Lord, please meet with me in whatever way you think fit."

One little tip. In our age of hyper-connectivity think very hard about taking electronic devices. It is so easy to be tempted to check social media, or to do a few quick emails. If you are used to reading your Bible on your phone or tablet, take a paper one with you. If you normally journal on your laptop, disable everything else so you aren't tempted by those incoming messages.

HOW CAN I BEST PREPARE?

Try to make sure you don't enter the day exhausted. Get some good night's sleep over the previous few nights. Identify what you are going to do over the weeks leading up to the day. Be sure that by the day before you've got a clear outline in your mind of passages you might read. There are a variety of ways to choose these. You could take the lectionary readings for the day, or simply choose some passages that you think may be helpful. Ask for others to pray for your day, that you may meet with God afresh. The night before, offer yourself to God in prayer, handing over the day to him and asking for his blessing.

HOW MIGHT SUCH A DAY BE SHAPED?

This is of course entirely up to you. Be sure not to overfill the day, and to allow space for relaxation and doing something recreational. Here is a pattern that I currently use as my template, and I then vary it each time.

9–9.15 Quieting down by acknowledging God's presence, offering yourself to him, and writing down any things that come crowding in that you need to take note of but are not a part of this day.

9.15–10.00 Read a predetermined passage of Scripture in a meditative way (I've found the Lectio Divina method pioneered by Ignatius really helpful). The aim of this time is not to prepare your next sermon or talk, but to ask God to meet with you and speak with you through the Scriptures.

10.00–10.30 Reflect on the meditation, perhaps by journaling, thinking on what has occurred. Here are some questions that might help in the journaling process.

- What went on? What struck me? How did I feel about this?

- What did God show me? Anything I need to do?

- Any recurring distraction?

- Is there some point to pick up in my next prayer time?

During the review thank God for his favours and ask forgiveness for sin. Throughout ponder what God may want you to do in your life.

- What is the next step in my relationship with God?

- What is the next step in the development of my character?

- What is the next step in my family life?

- What is the next step in my work?

10.30–11.30 Do something relaxing or creative. Go for a slow walk. Take notice of creation and allow God to speak to you through it. Paint, write poetry, compose a song, make something, write a Psalm, take photographs. In essence find a way that works for you of being creative, expressing something of what is in you to God, or allowing him to continue to feed you. Or if none of this works for you, read a book which engages you and helps you to reflect on your relationship with God.

11.45–12.15 Meditate on your second pre-chosen passage.

12.15–12.45 Reflect on your meditation.

12.45–1.45 Have a relaxed and leisurely lunch, or, if you are fasting, pray for the poor of the world.

1.45–2.15 Have a snooze. Go on – treat yourself. Alternatively get some gentle exercise.

2.15–3.30 Read something encouraging like a Christian biography or go for a slow reflective walk.

3.30–4.00 Reflect on the day as a whole perhaps asking:

- What do I sense God has been saying to me through this day?

- What might I need to do as a result of this day?

- How might I shape my daily life as a result of this day?

4.00 Day ends. If at all possible do something you really enjoy in the evening. Go to see a film, have a meal out with someone you love, go bowling, go to a concert... basically, have fun!

WHAT DO I DO IF THE DAY IS A REAL STRUGGLE?

We need to recognize that by placing ourselves entirely in God's hands we cannot govern the outcome of the day. Just because we have set aside a day to be spent in quiet with God doesn't mean it will necessarily be a spiritual high. That is why this is a discipline. God may well decide to hold himself back; because there are things he wants us to grapple with.

Quite often I find my quiet days are not much more than hard work. That is why it is really important to prayerfully plan the day in advance and then stick to it, thereby not allowing our feelings or tiredness to govern the agenda. It can also be really helpful to have a wise and godly spiritual director who you meet with two or three times a year to talk through your spiritual life, and perhaps share something of what happens on your quiet days.

HOW CAN I FIND OUT MORE?

Talk to older wiser Christians about their experience of setting aside time with God. In particular talk to those outside your tradition. You won't agree with everything they say, but you will gain valuable insights into how to spend time with God. You may also find the following books helpful:

- *Liberated to Lead*, Colin Buckland, Chapter 2 on Journaling (Kingsway)

- *The Life You've Always Wanted*, John Ortberg (Zondervan)

- *Seven Days of Solitude*, Brother Ramon (Liguori Publications)

TAKING A SABBATICAL

For those who are able to take a sabbatical it is a wonderful opportunity to recharge the batteries and do some wider stocktaking. I am very aware that many leaders are in roles where they aren't offered sabbatical leave, but even in those roles there may be creative ways to do something similar (in an earlier incarnation when I had few "responsibilities" I took four months leave between jobs, and a friend of mine working in business has recently been granted a six week period of extended leave).

The following are some of the things I have learnt in the process of taking two sabbaticals.

PLAN AHEAD

If you are thinking of taking a sabbatical recognize they can take up to two years to plan and to line up the various people who you need to make it happen (both those in authority over you, and those you work with) – so don't delay. Identify an ideal time of the year for you (it will vary, but a good rule of thumb is to try to take it over at least one of your "busy" periods), get the dates in the diary, and start approaching the people you need to approach.

In this period of planning:

- Don't be discouraged by negative or graceless comments: "Oh, it's alright for some." Do be humble and sensitive about how you communicate about it.

- Read everything you can on how to prepare for a sabbatical. There is lots of good material around. Some denominations have an officer responsible for sabbatical leave.

- Find someone to mentor or guide you through the process of going on sabbatical, from early thinking to taking it and then reflecting on it, someone who knows how to guide people through a sabbatical. I have had invaluable advice that has saved me from making some major mistakes.

- Prepare for it very thoroughly – practically, emotionally, and spiritually. You don't want to enter your sabbatical clueless about how to approach it. You will waste a lot of time. Identify a rhythm for your sabbatical that will serve you well.

BE CLEAR ABOUT WHAT YOU ARE TAKING

There is a difference between sabbatical and study leave. I know there are some technical reasons why, for example, Anglican dioceses tend to use study leave rather than sabbatical to describe them, but there is a difference. Study leave generally involves a project of some sort, a focus to the study that will lead to something at the end of it. Whilst this is a really good thing, and I think we ought to have study leave on a far more regular basis, sabbatical is not the same.

The focus of a sabbatical is rest, renewal, and recreation. The whole point is that there isn't necessarily a great project to do, but rather a great deal of space and non-pressured time to "be". Believe me, this is far more scary than a study break. It isn't that there aren't things that will be done on a sabbatical, but rather that there is an absence of pressure and the need to do "something".

BE PRAYERFUL

Try to distil the grace you are seeking from God during your sabbatical into a single sentence prayer. For example, on my first sabbatical it was "Lord, renew me in my relationship with you". Then pray that prayer and when others ask what they can pray for you, offer what you have discerned.

You can create a prayer card with that "grace" and with other key things on it, for example a retreat you are going on, and give it to people who ask what you are doing for your sabbatical.

BE PRACTICAL

Agree with colleagues terms of contact before you start. There is no right or wrong answer to this, but be very clear under what circumstances they are to break your sabbatical. They should be very few in number.

Sort what is going to happen to emails, post, and voicemail before you leave. The last thing you want is to return to a ridiculous mountain of emails and post. I put an automatic reply on my emails explaining I am on sabbatical, that all emails will be automatically deleted, and that if their email is urgent please resend to N. It is not good to continue to do work emails during a sabbatical, yet I am amazed how many times I have emailed people not knowing they were on sabbatical, only to receive a reply from them saying that "they are on sabbatical but in response to my email…" Some people set up a separate email account just for the period of their sabbatical and are careful about whom they give the address to.

I leave a message on voicemail explaining the same. And with post (not much these days) I ask a colleague to open it and sort it into three piles:

- Pile 1 is basically stuff I don't need to see. Straight in the rubbish bin.

- Pile 2 is stuff that they think I might be interested in, but can pick up at anytime.

- Pile 3 is the stuff that I need to give attention to as soon as I return.

RECOGNIZE THE "FLOW" OF A SABBATICAL

If at all possible, really do stop on the day your sabbatical starts. Try not to carry things over from work into the first week as all too often that then sets a pattern it is harder to stop. The first two weeks you will be really tired. Most of us end up working really hard to take the sabbatical just before it starts. So don't plan anything in those first two weeks. Slow down, chill, relax, do some fun things, and sleep lots.

A time of retreat is normally a good thing to do on a sabbatical (perhaps week two or maybe even better week three), as is a really special holiday. Build them in at appropriate points. Normally it takes around 4–8 weeks to realize how tired you are. Many speak of feeling a little depressed, down in the early parts. This is normal as you stop, and your body begins to recover from what is often years of overwork. For that reason it may be best to plan the holiday element for the latter part of the sabbatical when you are at your best and can most enjoy it.

Be sure to work out good patterns of exercise (ideally five to six times a week for at least thirty minutes, a simple walk is sufficient), of eating and drinking (all the normal stuff about your seven a day), and of sleeping (the hours before midnight really do count more than the ones after).

You may like to identify a hobby or area of interest that is not related to work that you would like to take up or reconnect with. For me it was photography. I bought myself a second-hand camera and learnt how to take some half decent photos. I had the space to give some time to this that simply wasn't available in normal life. Yet it was so energizing it has now become a part of normal life. What might the equivalent be for you?

Just as it takes time to get into a sabbatical, it is also helpful to take time to get out of it, otherwise it can be a fairly daunting experience of starting back on day one. The way I do that is by meeting with my mentor or spiritual director about ten days before the end of the sabbatical to help me process what has happened and what to do with what has happened. Then four or five days before I start back I gently plan for my re-entry. I ask for the pile three letters to be delivered to my home and sort them out. I look at my diary and plan for any meetings or events coming up in that first week. I re-engage my prayer life for my work. This only takes one or two hours a day, so it isn't returning to a full day, but just gently cranking back up. All this means that when I officially start back I am ready and I don't immediately feel lost in a sea of activity.

TAKE IT

And lastly, if you are in the privileged position to have a sabbatical – take one. There is something in the space that is immensely powerful. The opportunity to place ourselves in the hands of Almighty God for a set period in a way which just isn't possible in our normal roles is not to be missed. It is scary, but oh so worthwhile.

FOR FURTHER READING SEE:

- www.buildingchurchleaders.com – look at "Taking a Sabbatical", a series of articles and resources on sabbaticals.

- Google "clergy sabbaticals" for current diocesan advice (although this may contain elements of study leave).

- Look up *Best Practices for a Ministry Sabbatical* (Wheat Ridge Ministries), and *Sabbath Keeping and Sabbatical Taking* (Eastern North Dakota Synod Resource Center).

BIBLIOGRAPHY

The books below are listed in the order they appear in the book:

In the Name of Jesus, Henri Nouwen (DLT)

How to Survive and Thrive as a Church Leader, Nick Cuthbert (Monarch)

Zeal Without Burnout, Christopher Ash (Good Book Company)

Jesus Driven Ministry, Ajith Fernando (IVP)

Strengthsfinder 2.0, Tom Wrath (Gallup)

Working the Angles, Eugene Peterson (Eerdmans)

Good to Great, Jim Collins (Random House)

Building Below the Waterline, Gordon MacDonald (Hendrickson)

The Speed of Trust, Stephen Covey (CPAS)

Leading with Trust, Richard England (Grove Leadership Series No. 20)

Daring Greatly, Brene Brown (Penguin)

The Performance Factor, Pat MacMillan (Broadman and Holman)

The Leadership Challenge, James Kouzes and Barry Posner (Jossey Bass)

A Resilient Life, Gordon MacDonald (Thomas Nelson)

Don't Lose Heart, Graham Archer (Grove Leadership Series No. 16)

Encounters with Jesus, Timothy Keller (Hodder and Stoughton)

Finding Rest When the Work is Never Done, Patrick Klingaman (Charlot Victor)

Going the Distance, Peter Brain (Good Book Company)

Leaving Well, Andy Piggott (Grove Leadership Series No. 17)

Vulnerability in Leadership, Emma Sykes (Grove Leadership Series No. 24)

Engaging Gen Y, James Lawrence (Grove Leadership Series No. 8)

Discerning Leadership, Graham Cray (Grove Leadership Series No. 1)

First Break All the Rules, Marcus Buckingham and Curt Coffman (Simon and Schuster)

Beyond Busyness, Stephen Cherry (Sacristy Press)

Do It Tomorrow, Mark Forster (Hodder)

Busy Christian Living, Emma Ineson (Continuum)

The Busy Christian's Guide to Busyness, Tim Chester (IVP)

What's Best Next, Matt Perman (Zondervan)

Time for Everything, Matt Fuller (Good Book Company)

Ordering Your Private World, Gordon MacDonald (Thomas Nelson)

Insight into Stress, Bev Shepherd (Waverley)

Boundaries, Henry Cloud (Zondervan)

Unleashing the Power of Rubber Bands, Nancy Ortberg (Tyndale)

Facing Disappointment, James Newcome (Grove Leadership Series No. 25)

Thanks for the Feedback, Douglas Stone and Sheila Heen (Penguin)

Growing Leaders, James Lawrence (BRF)

Growing Young Leaders, Ruth Hassall (BRF)

Ready to Lead, Ruth Hassall (BRF)

Growing Leaders from Diverse Cultures – Leadership in a Multicultural Church, Andy Jolley (Grove Leadership Series No. 21)

All The Places to Go, John Ortberg (Tyndale)

Great by Choice, Jim Collins (Random House)

Crucial Conversations, Patterson, Grenny, McMillan, Switzler (McGraw Hill)

Transforming Conversation: How Jesus Talked to People, Rob Bewley (Grove Biblical Series No. 61)

Death by Meetings, Patrick Lencioni (John Wiley and Sons)

PCC Tonight, James Lawrence (CPAS)

Single Minded, Kate Wharton (Monarch)

Liberated to Lead, Colin Buckland (Kingsway)

The Life You've Always Wanted, John Ortberg (Zondervan)

Seven Days of Solitude, Brother Ramon (Liguori Publications)

BLOGS

There aren't many blogs I read regularly, but here are the ones I almost always read:

- Ian Paul's blog, subtitled "scholarship. serving. ministry.", covers a wide variety of topics relevant to those in leadership and offers a breadth of scholarship that is both stimulating and provocative at www.psephizo.com

- Chris Green's blog draws on his background as a biblical scholar, his academic interest in leadership, and the realities of working all of it out as a minister of a church: www.ministrynutsandbolts.com

Also worth taking a look at:

- Jules Middleton's blog that she started when she became a Christian in 2010 and which follows her journey through to ordination in 2016: www.pickingapplesofgold.com

- Leadership consultant to businesses and not for profits, Jonathan Wilson's posts on leadership by soul: leadbysoul.com/

- The monthly posts from the Arrow Leadership Programme in North America: www.sharpeningleaders.com/

- A blog focused on resourcing those involved with leadership amongst young people: www.youthworkhacks.com/blog

There are a wide and growing range of other Lead On articles like the ones contained in this book on the CPAS website: www.cpas.org.uk/leadon.